# HUNTING TRIPS IN THE CLASSROOM

Deborah A. Johnston

authorHOUSE®

*AuthorHouse™*
*1663 Liberty Drive*
*Bloomington, IN 47403*
*www.authorhouse.com*
*Phone: 1-800-839-8640*

*Published by AuthorHouse 2/14/2012*

*ISBN: 978-1-4678-7043-6 (e)*
*ISBN: 978-1-4678-7049-8 (sc)*

*Library of Congress Control Number: 2011962050*

*Any people depicted in stock imagery provided by Thinkstock are models, and such images are being used for illustrative purposes only.*
*Certain stock imagery © Thinkstock.*

*Cover illustration by:  Kennedy Kirby*

*This book is printed on acid-free paper.*

*Library of Congress Copyright Registration Number: TXu 1-674-057*
*Effective date of registration: February 22, 2010*

# HUNTING TRIPS IN THE CLASSROOM

BY: Deborah A. Johnston

Are you ready to go on a HUNT? I hope so! These hunts are a lot of fun, and they are educational. By spending fifteen to twenty minutes, you and your students will be able to do the following:

1) Learn about animals, including their descriptions, habitats, predators, diets, and babies.
2) Learn interesting facts about things, including geographical terrain and climate.
3) Touch on several subjects and skill sets, such as social studies, literacy, visualization, Bi-Lingual (foreign languages), and more.
4) Understand how you can apply classroom management to your classroom using the hunts for positive classroom behavior.
5) See how the Texas state testing module is aligned to the hunts.

There are sixteen hunts ready for your classroom. Enjoy them!

HAPPY HUNTING!

Deborah A. Johnston

# ACKNOWLEDGMENTS

Putting this teacher manual together was something I truly enjoyed doing. However, it was not done without a lot of encouragement and support. I would like to thank the following people who encouraged me to write this manual in so many ways.

<u>My wonderful family</u>
My husband, Randy: Not only did he support me, but he also came up with the title for this manual.
My children:

> Kara: She was the person who gave me the initial idea of *Hunting Trips in the Classroom*.
> Rachel: She gave me some great pep talks as I was going through the writing process.
> Matthew: He actually attended some of the hunts and gave me ideas as to what worked and what could be done differently.

My sister Donna: Not only did she support me, but she also helped with my initial editing.

My father, James: His support through this process was very much appreciated.

Other family and friends:

> Jean: She listened, read some of the hunts, and gave me support.
> Cindy: She got very excited, wanted to know more about the weekly hunts, and kept me going.

I also want to include my son-in-law, Jeremy, and my grandchildren Jameson and Brigitte as part of the dedication of this manual.

<u>My wonderful Pecan Creek Elementary coworkers</u>

Marci Kirby: Second-grade inclusion classroom teacher who has been right there from the beginning, encouraging me to practice the initial hunts in her classroom. She also encouraged me not to give up and to follow my dream of sharing these hunts with other teachers and families.

Jacqui Jenkins: Second-grade inclusion classroom teacher who welcomed weekly hunts in her classroom and encouraged me to move forward with my dream.

Jennifer Bautista: Third-grade inclusion classroom teacher who gave me many ideas for hunts and encouraged me to conduct hunts in her classroom.

Emily McLarty: Principal who encouraged me to follow my dream of being published.

Natalie Mead: Assistant principal who spoke to me about publishing books and encouraged me to never give up.

Rebecca Parker: Special education director at the Texas Education Centers who encouraged me to keep on with the dream.

Veronica Montes: Second-grade bilingual teacher who welcomed these hunts in her classroom and followed up with parents in getting permission for their children to be in a video demonstrating these hunts.

Cornelius Anderson: Encouraged me to continue writing this book and gave me the idea to include the Texas Essential Knowledge and Skills (TEKS), and edited them for me.

Countless others who have been there, listening and supporting me through this process.

# TABLE OF CONTENTS

# SUBJECTS/SKILL SETS

I found the hunts to be a fun way to touch on the following subjects and skill sets within a fifteen- to twenty-minute period:

- Bilingualism
- Social studies
- Science
- Literacy
- Speech
- Visualization
- Imagination

For the purpose of this manual, I used the TEKS for school year 2010–2011. Updated TEKS can be found at http://www.tea.state.tx.us/index.aspx.

# CLASSROOM MANAGEMENT TOOL

One thing we did for classroom management was require the students to, as a class, "earn" their invitations to the weekly hunts. The classroom teacher and I did this by giving them opportunities to earn two points each day. For example, if we had a five-day week, then they needed ten points. However, if we had only a four-day week, they needed eight.

We kept tally marks on the white board where all of the students could see the number of points they had at any given time.

Students had to work together and strive for 100 percent positive behavior. If they were asked to transition from their tables to the carpet, they had to do it in a manner that met our expectations. If they were able to do it, they earned a point. If not, they lost a point or didn't get one.

This is just one example of how classroom management was applied. It is helpful in getting positive-behavior participation from the students.

# HUNT STEPS

1) Fifteen minutes before the hunt is to begin, secretly meet with the student who chose the hunt and review information.

2) Have the rest of the students sit in a circle with their legs crossed.

3) The student who chose the hunt will stand in the middle of the circle, announce what the hunt is about, and share relevant animal information.
   a. The teacher stays in the middle with the student and has the information printed out in case the student needs to be reminded of something.

4) The student then joins the others in the circle.

5) The teacher asks students to close their eyes and tells them where they're going and what the animal looks, smells, and sounds like.

6) The teacher joins the students in the circle (sitting next to the student who chose the hunt) and asks students to open their eyes.

7) From that point, whatever the teacher says, the students say. Whatever actions the teacher does, the students do. The teacher follows the script.

8) Once the students find the animal, something (in the script) scares them, at which point they repeat all of the actions in reverse, going back to the beginning, where they end with kissing mom.

9) At that point, the hunt is over and the mimicking stops.

10) The student who led this hunt picks the next student.
   a. The teacher may want to have sticks with the students' names on them to draw from.

11) The teacher says, "Drum roll, please," and all of the students make a drum roll sound on the floor with their hands.

12) When the student picks a name, that person can accept or "pass" if he or she has already led one or would prefer not to do it.

13) All of the students go back to their seats except the student who will lead the next hunt.
   a. The teacher can give the student a choice of the prepared hunts or create one of their own. It's really a lot of fun!

14) The teacher meets with the student, who secretly tells the teacher what animal will be hunted next time.

15) The object of the hunt is kept a secret until the student reveals it at the time of the next hunt.

# HELPFUL HINTS FOR A SUCCESSFUL HUNT

To make the hunt more interesting, you might want to have the following available:

- pictures of the animal being hunted
- pictures of other animals that live in the same area
- pictures of the terrain
- a map or globe to show the students where in the world the animal lives
- visuals showing how large or small an animal is
  - o For example, I used another teacher who was around six feet tall
  - o I also used rulers or gave them reference points, such as "Visualize a school bus."

In addition, the Internet addresses in the Resource section are wonderful websites for gathering information. Also, make sure that you use inflection throughout the entire hunt.

# HOW TO ACT OUT THE HUNTS

Following is a list of actions used in the hunts, along with their descriptions. All actions are done while sitting down.

BBBBRRRRRRRRRR = Sound of a motorboat; put one hand behind you, as if you're steering a motorboat.

Bend down = Bend over your legs with your hands protecting your head.

BROOOMMM = Hold your hands up like you're driving a car and make the engine noise.

Check goggles = Put your hands up to your eyes like you're adjusting goggles.

Click = Hold your hands up like you're holding a camera and taking pictures.

Climb up = Using your hands, act as if you're climbing up a rock.

Climb down = Using your hands, act as if you're climbing down a rock.

Close door = Use your left hand and act like you're closing the door.

Close eyes = Cover your eyes with your hands or just close your eyes—your choice.

Close inner/outer gate = Same as Close door.

Get in boat = Act like you're jumping into a boat (hop while sitting).

Hand tickets to guide = Act like you have tickets in your hand and are giving them to someone in front of you.

Hop = Act like you're hoping while sitting.

Jump into jeep = Hop while sitting.

Jump out of jeep = Same as Jump in jeep.

Kick = Hold your hands straight out in front of you, palms down, and flick them up and down to simulate kicking.

Kiss Mom = Kiss the back of your hand.

Laugh = Just laugh.

Lean out = Act like you're hanging onto a mountain and leaning.

Listen = Cup your ear with your right hand like you're having a hard time hearing.

<u>Look</u> = Point to anywhere in the room.

<u>Look closer</u> = Put your hand flat over your eyebrows, like you're keeping the sun out of your eyes. Lean toward anywhere in the room.

<u>Open door</u> = Using your right hand, act like you're opening and walking out of the door.

<u>Open eyes</u> = If your eyes are covered, remove your hands from your eyes. If not, then just open your eyes wide.

<u>Open inner/outer gate</u> = Same as <u>Open door</u>.

<u>Pet</u> = Act like you're petting a dog or a cat.

<u>Pull back shade and look outside</u> = Using one hand, make it look like you're pulling back the shade to look outside a window.

<u>Put on clothes</u> = Act like you're putting clothes on.

<u>Quiver</u> = Act like you have the heebie jeebies and shiver.

<u>Reach</u> = Act like you're reaching for something in a boat or a drawer.

<u>Riding turtle</u> = Act like you're hanging onto the shell of a turtle, and act as if it's taking you on a roller coaster ride.

<u>Roll</u> = Roll your arms around in circles.

<u>Rub eyes</u> = Pretend that you're rubbing your eyes because you can't believe what you're seeing.

<u>RUMMMBBLLLEEE</u> = Act like you're riding in a jeep with your hands on the wheel and bump around a little, like the suspension is a little rough.

<u>Run</u> = Slap legs with open hands very quickly.

<u>Screech</u> = Act like you're in a jeep and stopping fast. Put your hands on the wheel, lean back, and say "Screech!"

<u>Scrunch</u> = Make noise as if you're walking on snow. Move fingertips on legs using a motion like opening a jar.

<u>Shake</u> = Act like you have the heebie jeebies and shiver. Same as <u>Quiver</u>.

<u>Sound like you're in water</u> = Put your hand up to your mouth and, with palms facing toward your face, wiggle your fingers and talk. It should sound like you're underwater.

<u>Splash</u> = Hold your nose and act like you're falling backward into the water from the boat and say "Splash!"

Squawk = Make a sound like a penguin.

Swim = With the tops of your hands facing each other, push out as if you're swimming in water while looking ahead. Continue as long as it feels comfortable to you.

Swim down = Same as Swim, but look down as well.

Swim up = Same as Swim, but look up as well.

Swish = Say "swish" and act like something just moved around under the brush.

Swoosh = With your hand flat and palms down, brush your hands across your lap.

Stop = Hold your right hand up in a stop position.

Tiptoe = Use your fingertips and touch your legs gently in a walking motion.

Turn around = Act like you're turning around to see what's behind you.

Turn off engine = Act like you're taking a key out of the ignition.

Turn on engine = Act like you're putting a key into the ignition.

Walking = Slap your legs with open hands, making a walking noise. Use your left hand and then your right hand.

# BLUE MOUNTAIN (RAINBOW) LORIKEETS

## DESCRIPTION

Type:           Bird from the parrot family.
Weight:         3.5–5.6 ounces
Height:         9–11 inches long
Color:          Head = dark purple-blue with yellow areas on the nape.
                Back of nape = reddish orange
                Chin = reddish orange
                Face = mostly reddish orange
                Back = lime green
                Tips of wings = lime green
                Under wing = black with yellow and green
                Chest = red with dark blue
                Belly = dark green
                Thighs = yellow green
                Upper tail = dark green with yellow tips
                Under tail = yellow and pink at the base
                Beak and irises = orange
                Legs = gray green
                Males and females look alike.
Intelligence:   Very smart
Texture:        Feathers
Tongue:         Featherlike
Movement:       Flies
Sight:          Good
Hearing:        Very good
Life span:      15–25 years in the wild

## HABITAT

Terrain:        Rain forests, woodlands, orchards
Climate:        Humid subtropical (hot, humid summers and cool winters)
Sleep:          Trees
Other animals:  Dingoes, kangaroos, emus, tiger snakes, brown falcons, pythons

## PREDATORS

Rainbow lorikeets need to be very careful because they are prey for brown falcons, whistling kites (bird), and pythons.

## DIET

Rainbow lorikeets will eat flowers (pansies, nasturtiums, roses, hibiscus, marigolds, and dandelions), pollen, nectar, seeds, insects, and some fruit. Because of their high energy, they need to eat a lot of food and spend most of the day eating.

## BABIES

Rainbow lorikeets usually have two or three white eggs in a clutch (a set of eggs during the nesting period). They will protect their eggs by keeping them in a tree cavity above the ground. The eggs are incubated by the female for a period of twenty-five to twenty-six days. With this species, the male will take care of the female by feeding her during the incubation period. After the chicks hatch, both parents will take care of them. The babies will stay with the parents for six to nine weeks before they're on their own.

## INTERESTING FACTS

- They like to eat their food in a very interesting way—they eat upside down.
- They are very busy birds, moving from tree to tree, collecting their food.
- Lorikeets like to be together, and it is not unusual to see a hundred of them together.
- They like to eat in groups of twenty.
- After getting used to an environment, they begin mimicking different sounds they hear.
- They are very good talkers and make great pets.
- They have *very high* energy.

# BLUE MOUNTAIN (RAINBOW) LORIKEETS HUNT

This hunt is going to take place on the Queensland Coast of Australia. All information and statistics come, verbatim, from the World Factbook (Central Intelligence Agency) website in September 2010:

| | |
|---|---|
| Continent: | Australia |
| Conventional long form: | Commonwealth of Australia |
| Conventional short form: | Australia |
| Population: | 21,262,641 (July 2010 est.) |
| Capital city: | Canberra |
| Languages: | English 78.5%, Chinese 2.5%, Italian 1.6%, Greek 1.3%, Arabic 1.2%, Vietnamese 1%, other 8.2%, unspecified 5.7% |
| Currency: | Australian dollar |
| Geographic coordinates: | 27° 00' S, 133° 00' E |
| Location: | Oceania, continent between the Indian Ocean and the South Pacific Ocean. |

## Students close their eyes, and the teacher explains what Queensland, Australia, looks like.

Think about a place that is pretty nice in January (their summer). The day temperature is normally in the mid to high seventies. Just imagine what you can see, like tall trees. You may even be able to hear the some of the wildlife, like dingoes barking.

## Students open their eyes, and the hunt begins.

(Pause between phrases for dramatic effect.)

Here we are, going on a hunt, except this time, we're taking a nice, "easy" hunt. Let's just walk around the beautiful area of Queensland, Australia. That's right! We're going to Australia to see the beautiful rainbow lorikeet. Now, we still have to be careful. We especially don't want to get in the way of any snakes like the tiger snake or brown snake. **QUIVER**

Okay, let's get ready:
Camera? Check.
Hat? Check.
Boots? Check.
Sunglasses? Check.
Walking stick? Check.
Water? Check.
Backpack? Check.
Okay, it's time to kiss my mom. Big, huge check!

I'm ready. How about you? You are? Well, let's go.

**OPEN DOOR/SHUT DOOR**

**WALK** Look at all of the great wilderness….I just *love* walking. Don't you? ….You do? ….That's great!

Do you know what? We're here in Australia, right? Well, I think we should speak with an Australian accent Don't you? Yes? Well, can you say, "G'day, mate"? Wow! That's neat I think we should keep speaking this way for the rest of the hunt!

**STOP** What was that? It's kind of tall, has a tail, cute ears, and a cute face. The face almost looks like a deer's. Wow! It looks like its tail is helping to keep it up. I know what *that* is. It's a kangaroo! Let's see if we can hop like a kangaroo. **HOP**

Okay, let's keep going. What's that? You want to take a picture? Sure, that's a good idea.

**CLICK** Okay, I think we're ready to keep on walking.

**WALK** Hey, what's *that*? It reminds me of an ostrich, but its neck isn't as long. It has a lot of feathers and long legs. Whoa! Did you see how fast those big birds ran? Those birds are called emus. I think we should keep on walking. I really want to find a rainbow lorikeet.

**WALK** Look over there! Those trees look pretty colorful. I wonder—do you think? Why don't we get a closer look.

**STOP** Look up. There they are! How beautiful! They look like rainbows that talk a lot. Wow! I'm taking a *lot* of pictures.

**CLICK** Okay, we found the lorikeets, and it's time to head back home.

**WALK** Hey, why are you hissing? What do you mean you're not hissing? I know I hear—uhhhhh. Oh, do you hear it too? You do? Well, that doesn't sound too good.

**STOP** Look over there. Do you see it? It is a tiger snake. I think we're getting in his way, and we should back away slowly. And now, we should *run!* **RUN**

---

To end the hunt, lead the students in repeating the movements in reverse order without talking. This must be done quickly, as if they're afraid they will be caught.

Then, end safely back at the start and give Mom a big kiss.

# EMPEROR PENGUIN

## DESCRIPTION

| | |
|---|---|
| Type: | Bird |
| Group Name: | Colony |
| Weight: | Up to 88 lbs |
| Height: | 45 inches |
| Color: | Lighter color on the belly and darker color on back and wings |
| Intelligence: | More instinctive than intelligent |
| Head: | Big |
| Tail: | Wedge-shaped |
| Feet: | Webbed |
| Wings: | Flipperlike |
| Texture: | So many feathers that you cannot feel their tummies |
| Movement: | Uses two legs to walk and run; webbed feet and flipperlike wings help them swim |
| Smell: | May have some sense of smell |
| Hearing: | Can hear very well |
| Sight: | Good eyesight |
| Life span: | 15–20 years in the wild |

Size relative to a six-foot man:
(NationalGeographic.com)

## HABITAT

| | |
|---|---|
| Terrain: | Ice lands |
| Climate: | Frigid |
| Sleep: | To protect themselves from their predators, they take small naps throughout the day. For further protection, and warmth, they will normally sleep in groups. |
| Other Animals: | Sea lions, leopard seals |

## PREDATORS

Leopard seals, sea lions, killer whales, birds of prey (eat eggs and chicks)

## DIET

Carnivore (meat eater)

The emperor penguin eats fish and squid; it will eat around three pounds of fish a day.


## BABIES

An interesting thing about emperor penguins is that the male will keep the newly laid egg warm. The egg is balanced on his feet and covered by a brood pouch (feathered skin). The male will do this until the female returns with food for the baby (can take up to two months). Once born, the chicks are taken care of by their mothers and are protected from the weather inside of the mother's brood pouch.

In December, the weather becomes warmer and open waters appear as the ice begins to break up. This happens at the time when the young are ready to fish and swim on their own.


## INTERESTING FACTS

-   They can see clearly on land and in water.

# EMPEROR PENGUIN HUNT

This hunt is going to take place in Antarctica. All information and statistics come, verbatim, from the World Factbook (Central Intelligence Agency) website in September 2010:

| | |
|---|---|
| Continent: | Antarctica |
| Conventional long form: | None |
| Conventional short form: | Antarctica |
| Population: | No indigenous inhabitants, but there are both permanent and summer-only staffed research stations |
| Capital city: | None |
| Languages: | None |
| Currency: | None |
| Geographic coordinates: | 90° S, 0.00° E |
| Location: | Continent mostly south of the Antarctic Circle |

## Students close their eyes, and the teacher explains what Antarctica looks like.

Think about a place with snow everywhere you look. It is very, very cold; actually, it is freezing. You can feel shivers from the cold, and your nose feels as if it's frozen. Listen closely and you may be able to hear the roar of a sea lion or maybe the squawking of emperor penguins.

## Students open their eyes and the hunt begins.

We're going on a hunt. It's going to be a *coooooold* hunt. Brrr! Where are we going? Why, to Antarctica, of course! What are we looking for? An emperor penguin, the biggest of the penguin species. Let's make sure we have everything we need.

Camera? Check.
Boots? Check.
Snowshoes? Check.
Big, warm coat? Check.
Scarf, hat, and gloves? Check.
Goggles? Check.
Kiss Mom? Check.

Okay, we're ready to go. Now, be very careful. It's very cold outside. Let's stick close together. Ready? Let's go.

**SCRUNCH SCRUNCH STOP** Do you know where we would find an emperor penguin? Well, I do. We have to keep walking until we get to the Ross Ice Shelf.

**SCRUNCH SCRUNCH STOP** This is taking *too* long. Let's get in our snowmobile.

**OPEN DOOR/SHUT DOOR/TURN KEY**

**BROOOMMM** Ah, that's better. Not so cold, too.

**BRUUUUUMMMM STOP** Oops, I think this is as far as we can go in our snowmobile. Ready to walk?

**TURN OFF THE ENGINE/OPENDOOR/SHUT DOOR**

**SCRUNCH SCRUNCH STOP** Wow! Look at all of the snow around here! It's like a winter wonderland. Let's take pictures. **CLICK** Okay, it's time to go.

**SCRUNCH SCRUNCH STOP** Look over there. There are some animals that look like they're wearing tuxedoes. Do you know what they are? I do. They're penguins! But not just *any* penguins. Those are emperor penguins. Let's get closer.

**SCRUNCH SCRUNCH STOP** Now, remember—do not touch the penguins. They don't like being picked up or touched. Let's just stand here and let them walk around us.

**SQUAWK SQUAWK** Did you hear that? That penguin walked right up to me and yelled at me! Do you know why? Because I was in his path and he had to walk around me. How funny. Let's take some pictures. **CLICK** I'd like to get a closer look at them diving into the water. Ready? Let's go.

**SCRUNCH SCRUNCH** Okay, I think if we get any closer we'll be swimming with the penguins! Wow! Look at them dive. It's great. I'm going to put my face closer to the water so I can see them underwater. I'd better make sure my goggles are on tight.

**CHECK GOGGLES** Now, let me look. Hey, I think I see something. Oh my! I think it's a leopard seal, and it looks a little hungry. Look at those spiky teeth! I think we're a little too close. Are you ready to run? **RUN**

---

To end the hunt, lead the students in repeating the movements in reverse order without talking. This must be done quickly, as if they're afraid they will be caught.

Then, end safely back at the start and give Mom a big kiss.

# GREAT WHITE SHARK

## DESCRIPTION

| | |
|---|---|
| Type: | Fish |
| Group name: | School or shoal |
| Weight: | 5,000 lbs. or more |
| Length: | 15–20 feet, sometimes longer |
| Color: | Gray on top and white underneath |
| Intelligence: | The are considered intelligent |
| Body: | Torpedo shaped |
| Tail: | Long and powerful |
| Mouth: | Have 300 serrated teeth that are in the shape of a triangle |
| Nose: | Used to track blood, not to breathe |
| Gills: | Used for breathing |
| Texture: | Scales that are rough like sandpaper |
| Movement: | Swims using tail at approximately 15 mph |
| Fins: | Six fins: first dorsal, second dorsal, caudal, anal, pelvic, and pectoral |
| Smell: | Remarkable sense of smell |
| Life span: | 30–100 years |

Size relative to a bus:
(NationalGeographic.com)

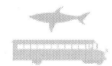

## HABITAT

| | |
|---|---|
| Found: | All over the world, except for Antarctica |
| Terrain: | Oceans and seas |
| Climate: | Warmer waters |
| Sleep: | Fish do not sleep like humans. They have what are called active and inactive periods. They may stay motionless during inactive periods or they may keep moving; it depends on the fish and how its breathing is affected. |
| Other animals: | Manatee, seals, sea lions, turtles, and whales |

## PREDATORS

Other than humans, sharks really aren't afraid of anything. It is a misunderstanding that sharks are afraid of dolphins. Dolphins will fight a shark and even kill it to protect their young, but other than that, they live very peacefully in the waters together.

## DIET

Carnivore (meat eater)

Great whites are known to be the biggest predators in the ocean. They will eat sea turtles, sea lions, seals, and carrion (dead animals). At times, sharks attack their prey from underneath. They have also been known to breach, which means that they get moving so quickly that they come out of the water to get their prey.

## BABIES

Females will migrate to warmer waters during the fall season in order to give birth to their babies. They are considered ovoviviparous, which means the eggs develop inside the mom until they are born. The pups develop very strong jaws within the first month after birth. The stronger pups will eat the weaker pups. They are usually born in the spring and summer months. They are on their own from birth.

## INTERESTING FACTS

- "Great whites can detect one drop of blood in 25 gal (100 L) of water and can sense even tiny amounts of blood in the water up to 3 mi (5 km) away." (nationalgeographic.com)
- "They get their name from their universally white underbellies." (nationalgeographic.com)

# GREAT WHITE SHARK HUNT

This hunt is going to take place on the island of Crete in Greece (Europe). All information and statistics come, verbatim, from the World Factbook (Central Intelligence Agency) website in September 2010:

| | |
|---|---|
| Continent: | Europe |
| Conventional long form: | Hellenic Republic |
| Conventional short form: | Greece |
| Population: | 10,737,428 (July 2010 est.) |
| Capital city: | Athens |
| Languages: | Greek 99%, other 1% includes English and French |
| Currency: | Euro |
| Geographic coordinates: | 39° 00' S, 22° 00' E |
| Location: | Southern Europe, bordering the Aegean Sea, Ionian Sea, and the Mediterranean Sea, between Albania and Turkey |

## Students close their eyes, and the teacher explains what Crete looks like.

We are going to Crete during the month of August, when the normal temperature is eighty-eight degrees, the weather sunny and warm. Look around this beautiful island; it's 155 miles long. There are caves, cliffs, beautiful blue waters, and beaches. Listen carefully and you can hear the water lapping onto the beach.

## Students open their eyes and the hunt begins.

Let's go on a great white shark hunt. Ready? Let's make sure we have everything we need.

Boogie board? Check.
Camera? Check.
Sunscreen on? Check.

OK, I am ready to go. Let's paddle out on our boogie boards.

**KICK STOP** Oh, no! Forgot something. I've got to go back and kiss my mom.

**KICK KISS** All right. I'm sure I've got everything now. Let's go.

**KICK STOP** Look over there. I see some monk seals. I can tell because they look like torpedoes— you know, like those big, huge bullets that come from submarines but with big eyes. Let's get closer.

**KICK** Wow! Look at them roll around. Let's roll like they do.

**ROLL STOP** This one looks curious. Let's see if it will let us pet it.

**PET** Oh, it's soft and fluffy like a cat.

**LAUGH** This seal just rubbed its whiskers against me! Let's take a picture.

**CLICK** Hey, where are the seals going? Let's follow them.

**KICK STOP** What's happening? The seals are swimming back toward us, fast. Wait a minute. What's that big thing coming out of the water? Did you see those teeth? Oh, my word! Those teeth belong to a great white shark! Yikes! Let's get out of here *fast!*

---

To end the hunt, lead the students in repeating the movements in reverse order without talking. This must be done quickly, as if they're afraid they will be caught.

Then, end safely back at the start and give Mom a big kiss.

# HAMMERHEAD

## DESCRIPTION

Type:           Fish
Group name:     School or shoal
Weight:         500–1,000 pounds
Length:         13–20 feet
Color:          Gray-brown to olive-green on top; off-white on bottom
Intelligence:   Very intelligent
Head:           Rectangle (hammer-shaped)
Fins:           Extra tall and pointed
Texture:        Smooth, leathery feel
Movement:       Swims
Sight:          Excellent
Smell:          Excellent
Taste:          Uses its long, yellow, forked tongue
Hearing:        Not very good
Life span:      20–30 years in the wild

Size relative to a six-foot man:
(NationalGeographic.com)

## HABITAT

Located:        "Hammerheads are found worldwide in warmer waters along coastlines and continental shelves." (Wikipedia.org)
Terrain:        Tropical
Climate:        Warmer waters during the winter and cooler waters during the summer
Sleep:          There isn't any evidence that these sharks sleep.
Other animals:  Stingrays, octopuses, squid, other sharks, marlins, crabs, shrimp, spearfish, swordfish

## PREDATORS

Orca whales are predators of the hammerhead shark. It has been said that hammerheads are afraid of dolphins, but this is not entirely true. Dolphins and hammerheads have to compete for the same food, but if they or their babies are threatened, the dolphin will attack the hammerhead shark.

## DIET

Carnivore (meat eater)

They will eat fish such as stingrays (seem to be their favorite), sharks, squid, octopuses, and crustaceans.

## BABIES

The young are born alive, with the mother giving birth anywhere from twelve to fifteen pups. However, if looking at the Great Hammerhead, the mother will give birth anywhere from twenty to forty pups. The pups are approximately twenty-seven inches long when they're born.

## INTERESTING FACTS

- "Hammerheads use their wide heads to attack stingrays, pinning the winged fish against the sea floor." (NationalGeographic.com)
- "Hammerheads are notably one of the few animals that acquire a tan from prolonged exposure to sunlight." (Wikipedia.org)

# HAMMERHEAD HUNT

This hunt is going to take place in Kona, Hawaii, during the month of October. All information and statistics come, verbatim, from the World Factbook (Central Intelligence Agency) as well as the US Census Bureau websites in September 2010:

| | |
|---|---|
| Continent: | North America |
| Conventional long form: | United States of America |
| Conventional short form: | United States |
| Population: | 1,295,178 |
| State: | Hawaii |
| Capital city: | Honolulu |
| Languages: | Hawaiian (official), English |
| Currency: | US dollar |
| Geographic coordinates: | 19° 45' N, 155° 45' W |
| Location: | Hawaii is located in the Pacific Ocean, west of the Continental US |

## Students close their eyes, and the teacher explains what Kona, Hawaii looks like.

Think about a warm tropical place where you can see coconuts in the trees. Everywhere you look, you can see beautiful, colorful flowers. If you breathe in, you can smell the sweet flowers and salt from the ocean water. You can hear the ocean waves crashing on the beach.

## Students open their eyes and the hunt begins.

Are you ready for a wonderful hunt? Guess where we are. We're in Hawaii! To be more specific, we're in Kona, Hawaii. What are we going to hunt? How about a hammerhead shark? Do you like the boat we're using? Well, we'd better get going.

**BBBBRRRRRRRRRR STOP** We're here! Let's make sure we have everything we need before diving.

Rubber suit? Check.
Oxygen tank? Check.
Flippers? Check.
Goggles? Check.
Kiss my mom? Check.

Looks like we're ready to go! Let's get into the water.

**SPLASH SWIM DOWN** (Sound like you're talking underwater) Oops! Forgot something. I need to go back to the surface and get my camera.

**SWIM UP REACH** Got my camera. Ready to go.

**SWIM DOWN** Let's look for some coral first. Ooohh, it's pretty and all different colors. Let's take a picture.

**WAIT** Oh, my! What's that going in and out of the coral? Why, it looks like a clown fish, just like the one in Disney's *Finding Nemo*. Let's take a picture. **CLICK** Let's keep going.

**SWIM STOP** Look over there. It looks like a fish that is blue and yellow. Oh, wow! It's a mahi-mahi. How cool! Let's take another picture. **CLICK** Okay, let's keep on going. We need to find a hammerhead shark.

**SWIM** Wow! Look over there! I think there's a big sea turtle. Let's catch a ride like they did in *Finding Nemo*.

**RIDING TURTLE** That was fun, but we need to keep looking for a hammerhead.

**SWIM** I wonder if there are any dolphins around here. Hey, wait. I think I just saw one. I know they like humans. Let's swim over and pet one.

**PET DOLPHIN** I really liked that one! We still need to find our hammerhead, though.

**SWIM** Look over there! It's a barracuda. We need to stay very still. Let's hope it just swims past us. Phew! That was a close one! Let's keep looking; I know there's a hammerhead shark somewhere around here.

**SWIM STOP** What is that swimming above us? I think I'm seeing a hammer swimming around. Hey, wait a minute I think that may be a hammerhead shark! We found it! Yeah! Uh-oh. I think we'd better go because he's looking right at us. Don't make a move until I say so. Ready? OK. Swim as fast as you can! **SWIM**

---

To end the hunt, lead the students in repeating the movements in reverse order without talking. This must be done quickly, as if they're afraid they will be caught.

Then, end safely back at the start and give Mom a big kiss.

# OCTOPUS

## DESCRIPTION

Type:            Invertebrate
Weight:          6.6–22 lbs.
Length:          12–26 inches
Color:           Varies; color changes to blend into surroundings
Intelligence:    Highly intelligent
Head:            Large and round
Legs:            Eight long legs with suction cups
Mouth:           Parrotlike beak
Texture:         Can change depending on environment; can be smooth or pointy
Movement:        Swims with a jet propulsion caused by spewing water from its body; also uses legs to crawl and swim at a normal pace.
Touch:           Suction cups have sensors (they also allow the octopus to taste)
Smell:           Can smell
Hearing:         Can hear
Sight:           Sharp eyesight
Life span:       6 months–2 years

Size relative to a six-foot man:
(NationalGeographic.com)

## HABITAT

Located:        Coral reefs all over the world
Terrain:        Oceans and seas
Climate:        Warmer waters
Sleep:          Will sleep in dens (caves), spaces under rocks, crevices on the sea floor, or holes they dig under large rocks
Other animals:  Moray eels, mollusks, scallops, crabs, snails, turtles

## PREDATORS

They will pile rocks to block the openings to their dens, protecting themselves from predators. Predators include moray eels and other octopuses. They also remove themselves from difficult situations by spurting out a black ink, which obscures them from view and gives them time to escape.

## DIET

Carnivore (meat eater)

Their main course will include small crabs, scallops, some snails, fish, turtles, and other octopuses. After they have captured their prey (using their arms, of course), they kill it by biting it with their tough beaks. This paralyzes their prey with nerve poison, which also softens the flesh. After that, they use their beak to dismember their prey into smaller pieces. They hunt mostly at night, and they have been known to spurt their black ink to confuse their prey and make it easier to capture them.

## BABIES

A mother octopus protects her eggs for one to two months and does not eat during that time. She piles rocks to block her den, which provides a safe place to put her eggs.

## INTERESTING FACTS

- "Common octopuses will collect crustacean shells and other objects to construct fortresses, or 'gardens,' around their lairs." (NationalGeographic.com)
- Octopuses have blue blood.
- The word *octopus* means "eight feet."

# OCTOPUS HUNT

This hunt is going to take place in Miami, Florida. All information and statistics come, verbatim, from the World Factbook (Central Intelligence Agency) as well as the US Census Bureau websites in September 2010:

| | |
|---|---|
| Continent: | North America |
| Conventional long form: | United States of America |
| Conventional short form: | United States |
| State: | Florida |
| Capital city: | Tallahassee |
| Population: | 18,537,969 (2009 est.) |
| Languages: | English 82.1%, Spanish 10.7%, Indo-European 3.8%, Asian and Pacific Island 2.7%, other 0.7% (2000 census) |
| Currency: | US dollar |
| Geographic coordinates: | 25° 48' N, 80° 16' W |
| Location: | North America bordering both the North Atlantic Ocean and the North Pacific Ocean, between Canada and Mexico. In the United States of America, Florida shares a border with Alabama and Georgia. Being a peninsula, it is surrounded by the Atlantic Ocean as well as the Gulf of Mexico. |

## Students close their eyes, and the teacher explains what Florida looks like.

Think about seeing palm trees all around. Listen and you can hear the ocean splash on the beach. You can see something—pink flamingoes flying in the air or maybe standing on one leg. The air is warm, and it is humid.

## Students open their eyes and the hunt begins.

We're going to stay close to home on this hunt We're going to Miami, Florida, where the coral reefs are. It is such a pretty place to go, but we have to be in the water and swim to the ocean floor. Are you ready? Let's get started and get into our boat

**BBBBRRRRRRRRRR STOP** Here is a good place to start our hunt. Let's make sure we have everything we need.

Rubber suit on? Check.
Oxygen tank filled and ready to go? Check.
Put my goggles on? Check.
Kiss my mom? Check. Let's go!

**SPLASH SWIM DOWN** (sound like you're talking under water) Oops! Forgot something. I have to go back to the surface and get my camera.

**SWIM UP REACH** Okay, got my camera. Are you ready? Set? Let's go.

**SWIM DOWN** (sound like you're talking under water) Let's look for some coral first. Ooh, it's pretty and all different colors. Let's take a picture. **CLICK** Wow! What's that over there? It looks like a flat snake. Oh, that's a moray eel. Creepy, but—do you know what? Yep. Another picture opportunity. **CLICK** Okay, let's keep going. I want to find an octopus.

**SWIM STOP** Look over there. Do you see that school of fish? Let's see, they are greenish on the top and silvery toward their belly. There have round black spots on their backs that go all of the way to it's tail. I think I remember what these fish are – they are called Spotted Seatrout and they usually weigh around 4 lbs fully grown, but guess what? There was one, found in Florida, that weighed over 15 lbs. What a record! Let's take another picture. **CLICK** Let's keep looking for our octopus.

**SWIM STOP** Look over there. It kind of looks like a spider with a big, round head, two huge eyes, and eight legs. But wait—I don't remember any swimming spiders in my research. Let's get closer.

**SWIM STOP** Wow! I think we're close enough to look at those legs. They have suction cups on them. Wait a minute. That's not a spider! It's an octopus. Do you think we should get closer? Yes, let's. Ready?

**SWIM STOP** Whoa! That octopus sprayed some black stuff at us. I wonder why. Well, let's get a little closer.

**SWIM STOP** Oh, no! I think that black ink was a warning because now we have made the octopus angry. How do I know? Well, look at what's coming at us! Let's get out of here! **SWIM FAST**

---

To end the hunt, lead the students in repeating the movements in reverse order without talking. This must be done quickly, as if they're afraid they will be caught.

Then, end safely back at the start and give Mom a big kiss.

# AFRICAN ELEPHANT

## DESCRIPTION

| | |
|---|---|
| Type: | Mammal |
| Group name: | Herd |
| Weight: | 5,000–14,000 lbs. |
| Height: | 8.2–13 feet at the shoulder |
| Color: | Brown/gray |
| Intelligence: | Very intelligent |
| Head: | Large with two huge ears that resemble Africa (ears measure up to five feet long) |
| Nose: | Very long and called a trunk, containing 100,000 muscles |
| Mouth: | Two large teeth called tusks, and four molars |
| Feet: | Five toes and nails on front legs and five toes and three nails on back legs |
| Tail: | About four feet long with hair at the end |
| Texture: | Thick, wrinkled skin that is almost hairless |
| Movement: | Walks and runs on four legs |
| Touch: | With their trunks |
| Smell: | Excellent |
| Hearing: | Excellent |
| Sight: | Not very good |
| Life span: | 70 years |

Size relative to a six-foot man:
(NationalGeographic.com)

## HABITAT

| | |
|---|---|
| Terrain: | Grasslands, lakes, tropical rain forests and savannas |
| Climate: | The climate can vary. The coastal regions and islands are humid with inland being dry. The temperature can be anywhere from the sixties to the eighties, except the high mountains, which are freezing near the top. |
| Sleep: | Elephants will sleep on the ground on one side for approximately thirty minutes, get up, eat, and then lay down on the other side for thirty minutes. They do not sleep very soundly and are always alert. If they hear a strange noise, they wake right away and remain awake. |
| Other animals: | Lions, pumas, meerkats, monkeys, and giraffes |

## PREDATORS

Packs of desperate lions have been known to take down elephants (only when the elephant is alone), but this is not common. Their true predators, I'm sorry to say, are humans.

## DIET

Herbivore (plant eater)

Adult elephants can eat up to three hundred pounds of food each day. Their diet includes roots, grasses, fruit, and bark.

## BABIES

Having babies is very important to elephants. Cows (females) will carry one calf for almost twenty-two months before giving birth. When born, calves weigh approximately two hundred pounds and are about three feet tall.

## INTERESTING FACTS

- "Elephant ears radiate heat to help keep these large animals cool, but sometimes the African heat is too much." (NationalGeographic.com)
- Male elephants are called bulls, and females are called cows.

# AFRICAN ELEPHANT HUNT

This hunt is going to take place in Nairobi, Kenya. All information and statistics come, verbatim, from the World Factbook (Central Intelligence Agency) website in September 2010:

Continent:                      Africa
Conventional long form:         Republic of Kenya
Conventional short form:        Kenya
Population:                      39,002,772
Capital city:                   Nairobi
Languages:                      Swahili and English (both official) and numerous indigenous languages
Currency:                       Kenya shilling
Geographic coordinates:         1°00'S, 38°00'E
Location:                       Eastern Africa, bordering the Indian Ocean, between Somalia and Tanzania

## Students close their eyes, and the teacher explains what Nairobi looks like.

Think about seeing grasslands with trees and shrubs sprinkled here and there. Think about how hot and dry it is. Can you hear the sounds of a zebra braying or perhaps a lion roaring. Could there be some hyenas cackling?

## Students open their eyes and the hunt begins.

Here we are in Nairobi, Kenya, a country in Africa, to find an African elephant. Do you know that an African elephant can weigh up to fourteen thousand pounds? That's seven tons! Yikes! I think we'd better be very careful on this hunt! Well, let's get going. We need to make sure we have everything we need.

Camera? Check.
Hats? Check.
Sunglasses? Check.
Water? Check.
How about my backpack? Check.
Let's not forget to kiss Mom. Huge, big elephant check!

Let's go.

**OPEN DOOR/SHUT DOOR**

**WALK OPEN INNER GATE/SHUT INNER GATE**

**WALK OPEN OUTER GATE/SHUT OUTER GATE**

**WALK** Oh, look over there. Let's get in our jeep. Ready?

**JUMP IN THE JEEP**

**RUMMMBBLLLEEE STOP** I think my eyes are playing tricks on me. I think I see something black and white running. Let's get a little closer.

**RUMMMBBLLLEEE** The last time I saw something black and white, it was an emperor penguin. I don't think this a penguin, though. The weather is too warm. Oops, just a little closer. Wow! Watch those horses gallop. But wait! Those aren't horses. Those are zebras! Man, can they fun fast! But, they're not elephants, so let's keep looking.

**RUMMMBBLLLEEE STOP** Oh, my! Let's get out for just a minute. I see something kind of—well, how can I explain it? This animal has very long legs plus a very long neck. I remember seeing this animal in a zoo once. I think it is a giraffe. Yuck! Did you see that? It stuck out its tongue to grab some leaves off of that tree. I think that is the longest tongue I have ever seen in my life! However, it might make a good picture. Ready? **CLICK** OK, let's keep going. I really want to find an African elephant. Ready? Let's go.

**RUMMMBBLLLEEE** Look over there I see a lot of water, and I also see something rolling around in it. Oh, my! I have got to stop! **STOP** Why? Because I think I found an African elephant!

**WALK WALK** Yes! It *is* an African elephant! Wow! Those are pretty big animals! Look at the cute calf holding onto its mom's tail. Do you know what? I think the baby calf is even bigger than I am. I think we should be careful.

**LOOK CLOSER** Look over there. I wonder why that elephant isn't near the rest of the herd. Uh-oh! Something is spooking it, and it is starting to run toward us! Wait. I see what is spooking it! There's a pack of lions chasing it! Oh, no! I think we'd better get going if we don't want to be trampled, so let's run really fast! **RUN**

---

To end the hunt, lead the students in repeating the movements in reverse order without talking. This must be done quickly, as if they're afraid they will be caught.

Then, end safely back at the start and give Mom a big kiss.

# AMERICAN BISON

## DESCRIPTION

Type:            Mammal
Group name:      Herd
Weight:          900–2,000 pounds
Height:          About six feet tall
Length:          Ten feet long
Color:           Dark brown coat in the winter and light brown coat in the summer
Intelligence:    Very intelligent
Head:            Massive with sharp, curved horns that can grow up to two feet long
Tail:            Long (around twenty inches)
Feet:            Hooves
Legs:            Short
Texture:         Shaggy forequarter with shorter, finer hair on the rest of the body
Movement:        Walks and runs on four legs
Sight:           Poor
Smell:           Excellent sense of smell
Hearing:         Acute hearing
Life span:       Twelve to twenty years in the wild

Size relative to a six-foot man:
(NationalGeographic.com)

## HABITAT

Terrain:         Wooded, close to streams
Climate:         In the wintertime, temperatures stay below freezing. During the spring, it gets warmer. In the summer, highs are in the sixties and seventies.
Sleep:           They will sleep in their herd or when they can find shelter from the environment. One bison will keep watch while the herd is sleeping.
Other animals:   Moose, grizzly bears, pronghorn antelope, deer, coyote, wolf, trumpeter swans, eagles, elk, coyotes, wolves

## PREDATORS

Aside from humans, bison have very few enemies. On occasion, adult bison have been attacked and killed by a pack of wolves. The young may be killed by grizzly bears and wolves. These kinds of attacks normally happen during the winter months when the herd cannot use a lot of energy to protect those who fall behind.

## DIET

Herbivore (plant eater)

They are known as grazers. Their diet includes grasses, shrubs, and twigs. An interesting thing about their digestive system is that they swallow their food whole and, at a later time, regurgitate it and chew it as cud before digesting the food.

## BABIES

Mothers give birth to one calf at a time, usually during the spring. They are lighter in color (usually reddish-brown) during their first three months. Calves are considered mature when they reach the age of three years.

## SAFETY

The best thing to do when you see a bison is to stay away and not approach it. They will not bother you unless they feel threatened.

## INTERESTING FACTS

- "The bison's thick, shaggy coat is so well insulated that snow can settle on its back without melting." (NationalGeographic.com)
- Females are called cows and males are called bulls.
- "Bison can run at speeds up to 30 mph." (Enchanted Learning)
- Another name for the American bison is buffalo.
- "In winter, bison can dig through deep snow with their heads to reach the vegetation below." (Defenders of Wildlife)

# AMERICAN BISON HUNT

This hunt is going to take place in Yellowstone National Park in Wyoming in the month of June. All information and statistics come, verbatim, from the World Factbook (Central Intelligence Agency) as well as the US Census Bureau websites in September 2010:

Continent:                         North America
Conventional long form:            United States of America
Conventional short form:           United States
State:                             Wyoming
Capital city:                      Cheyenne
Population:                        544,270 (2009 est.)
Languages:                         English 82.1%, Spanish 10.7%, Indo-European 3.8%, Asian and Pacific Island 2.7%, other 0.7% (2000 census)
Currency:                          US dollar
Geographic coordinates:            38° 00' N, 97° 00' W
Location:                          North America bordering both the North Atlantic Ocean and the North Pacific Ocean, between Canada and Mexico. Wyoming is south of Montana, east of Idaho, northeast of Utah, north of Colorado, northeast of Nebraska and southeast of South Dakota

## Students close their eyes, and the teacher explains what Yellowstone National Park looks like.

Think about a place that has a lot of beautiful trees and mountains. You can see steam coming from geysers and hear the water bubbling. Listen carefully and you may be able to hear waterfalls and fast-moving water in streams. You can see animals such as moose, deer, and bison, and perhaps you can see a beautiful eagle flying above you.

## Students open their eyes and the hunt begins.

We're going on an American bison hunt. Do you know another name for the American bison? They're also called buffalo. Guess where we're going. To Yellowstone National Park, where the buffalo run free Ready? Let's make sure we have everything we need.

Camera? Check.
Hat? Check.
Good hiking boots? Check.
Walking stick? Check.
Binoculars? Check.
Don't forget to kiss mom! Check.

Let's start by getting in the car.

**OPEN DOOR/CLOSE DOOR**

**BROOOMMM STOP** Here we are. Wait a minute. Where is all of that steam coming from? Let's go check it out. Ready? Let's drive.

**BROOOMMM STOP** There it is. Let's get out and get a closer look.

**OPEN DOOR/CLOSE DOOR**

**WALK** Wow! That's neat. It looks like bubbling water. It *is* bubbling water. The guide said it's bubbling because we're actually standing on top of a volcano! Let's get a closer look. Wait! Not *that* close! We have to stay on the walkway so we don't get hurt. Hey, let's take a picture. **CLICK** I'm ready to go find some buffalo. Let's go back to our car.

**WALK OPEN DOOR/CLOSE DOOR**

**BROOOMMM STOP** Look at that animal. What is that? It looks kind of like Bambi's mom and dad. And look over there! That one looks like Bambi. do you know what they are? They're deer! *So* cute, but I still want to find some buffalo. Let's keep driving.

**BROOOMMM STOP** I see some water shooting into the air. I want to see what it is. Ready?

**BROOOMMM** Let's find a good parking spot. Oh, there's one.

**EERRRKKK** Okay, we're parked. Why are so many people standing over there? Let's walk over and find out.

**WALK STOP** Whoa! What was that? Why, it's a geyser! Let's listen to what the guide is saying. He says this geyser is called Old Faithful, and they call it that because it shoots up water every twenty-seven minutes. Let's take another picture. Uh-oh. Guess what? I left my camera in the car. Let's go get it.

**WALK** Here it is. Okay, I'll keep it around my neck this time. Oh, I'm hearing some bubbling noises! Let's run over to Old Faithful so we don't miss it.

**RUN STOP** Look at that! The water is going up very high. Watch out! It's scalding hot. The guide said that the water went up seventy-five feet this time. Take a picture! **CLICK** Okay, let's go and find some buffaloes! We need to get back in the car.

**WALK OPEN DOOR/CLOSE DOOR**

**BROOOMMM STOP** I see—well, I *think* I see … Yes! I found the buffaloes! Let's get out and get a little closer.

**WALK WHISPER** Be very careful. If we get too close, he might chase after us. If he catches us, he might use his horns to flip us!

**TIPTOE** I've got to take a picture. Ready? **CLICK** Oh, no! I don't think he liked hearing the clicking sound from the camera. I think it's time to run! **RUN**

---

To end the hunt, lead the students in repeating the movements in reverse order without talking. This must be done quickly, as if they're afraid they will be caught.

Then, end safely back at the start and give Mom a big kiss.

# CHEETAH

## DESCRIPTION

Type:            Mammal
Weight:         75–150 lbs.
Length:         4.3–4.9 feet (tail is an additional 2 to 2.5 feet)
Height:         2.3–2.8 feet from shoulder to ground.
Color:          Tan with about 2,000 small round black spots; black "tear marks" run from the corners of the eyes down the side of the nose to the mouth.
Intelligence:    Very intelligent
Head:          Small head
Claws:          Semiretractable claws that are blunt
Texture:        Fur is coarse and short
Movement:     Walk and sprints on four legs
Smell:          Very good sense of smell
Hearing:        Acute hearing
Taste:          Tongue textured like sandpaper
Life span:      15 years in a zoo or 12 years in the wild.

Size relative to a six-foot man:
(NationalGeographic.com)

## HABITAT

Located:        Africa and Southwestern Asia
Terrain:        Wide-open grasslands known as savannas and semi-deserts
Climate:       Dry and hot
Sleep:         In brush or tall grass and under trees; can sleep twelve to thirteen hours at night and may nap during the day.
Other animals: African wild dogs, meerkats, lions, hyenas, gazelles, and ostriches.

## PREDATORS

Predators include humans, lions, jaguars, and hyenas. Another predator that is a danger to the cubs (for the first three months) is the eagle.

## DIET

Carnivore (meat eater)

Cheetahs will eat birds, gazelles, rabbits, and ostriches. They can eat up to six pounds of food each day. They get their food by running and using their claws to catch and take down their prey.

## BABIES

They will have a litter of three cubs. The cubs will stay with their mother for approximately two and a half years, with the first year spent learning how to hunt.

## INTERESTING FACTS

- "Cheetahs can run up to 70 mph, which make them the fastest cat/mammal. They cannot run that fast for a long period of time, which is why they're called sprinters." (NationalGeographic. com)
- "Cheetahs do not need a lot of water and drink once every 3–4 days." (NationalGeographic. com)
- The black "tear marks" on the cheetah's face keep the sun out of its eyes and aid in hunting.
- Cheetahs are on the endangered species list.
- They use their sense of smell to detect where other cheetahs have marked their territory by urinating on tree trunks.
- "Cheetahs come from the Hindu word *chita* which means 'spotted one'" (exzooberance. com)

# CHEETAH HUNT

This hunt is going to take place in Namibia, Africa, between August and October. Statistics come from the World Factbook (Central Intelligence Agency) in September 2010:

Continent:                          Africa
Conventional long form:             Republic of Namibia
Convention short form:              Namibia
Population:                          2,108,665
Capital city:                        Windhoek
Languages:                           English 7% (official), Afrikaans 60%, German 32% and 1% indigenous (includes Oshivambo, Hereto and Nama); numerous tribal dialects
Currency:                            Namibian dollar
Geographic coordinates:             22° 00' S, 17° 00' E (Windhoek)
Location:                            Southern Africa bordering the South Atlantic Ocean, between Angola and South Africa

## Students close their eyes, and the teacher explains what Namibia looks like.

Think about a place that feels a lot like Arizona. It is very hot and dry and feels cooler in the shade. There are trees and shrubs strewn throughout the rolling grassland. Listen carefully and you might hear the roar of lions and see eagles flying in the air.

## Students open their eyes and the hunt begins.

Why, hello there! I bet I know what you're ready for. Yep, a great hunt! Yes! We are headed for the wilds of the African savanna, where the cheetahs roam free. Actually, we're going to Namibia, Africa. It is such a neat place to find cheetahs and maybe other kinds of animals as well. Are you ready? Oops. I don't know about you, but I'm not. Let's see. What will I need?

Camera? Check.
Long-sleeved shirt? Check.
Socks? Check. (We don't want to get insect bites.)
Sunglasses? Check.
Hat and sunscreen? Check.
Good hiking boots? Check.
Binoculars? Check.
Most importantly, kiss Mom? Check.

Okay, I think we're ready to go. Guess what? We're going to go on an actual safari! Are you excited? I know I am. Let's get in the jeep. Our guide is waiting for us.

**RUN TO THE JEEP/HOP IN THE JEEP**

**RUMMMBBLLLEEE STOP** Wait. The guide stopped the jeep. I wonder why? Oh, I can see now. Look over there. It looks like a raccoon, but it's actually called a meerkat. It's from the mongoose family—you know, like Timone in Disney's *The Lion King*. Wow, there are a lot of them over there! Do you know why they stand up like that and stay in a group? They are warning us to not get too close. I think we should listen and keep our distance. But will that stop us from taking a picture? Of course not! **CLICK** Our guide is ready to move on. Let's go.

**RUMMMBBLLLEEE STOP** Oops, looks like we're stopping again. Our guide is pointing to something way out there. I can't really make those animals out. I think it's time to get out our trusty binoculars. Look through. Wow! Now I know why our guide didn't want to get too close. Can you see the pack of African wild dogs? Did you know that they are on the endangered species list? I think we should let them go on about their business. Do you agree? You do? Well, let's go until we find a cheetah.

**RUMMMBBLLLEEE** Wow, look at those tall trees. Hey, let's get a closer look at those trees.

**RUMMMBBLLLEEE STOP** I think I see something. Wait. Yes, I see a cheetah! It's resting up in the tree. Let's look through our binoculars to get a closer look.

**LOOK** I think it's looking a little hungry. Not only that, but I think it's looking at us. Do you think we would make a tasty meal? No? I have to agree with you, so Mr. Guide, please get us out of here now! Because here it comes! Wow! They can run fast! Let's go!

---

To end the hunt, lead the students in repeating the movements in reverse order without talking. This must be done quickly, as if they're afraid they will be caught.

Then, end safely back at the start and give Mom a big kiss.

# GRIZZLY BEAR

## DESCRIPTION

Type:            Mammal
Weight:          1,500 lbs. (with the females about two thirds the size of the males)
Height:          5–8 feet tall
Color:           Dark brown fur that sometimes appears to have white tips
Intelligence:    Very intelligent
Head:            Large head with small, rounded ears
Tail:            Short
Claws:           Front claws (4.75 inches) longer than back claws (2.2 inches)
Texture:         Coarse and long fur
Movement:        Walks and runs on two or four legs
Smell:           Very good sense of smell
Hearing:         Acute hearing
Taste:           Tongue textured like sandpaper
Life span:       Twenty-five years in the wild

Size relative to a six-foot man:
(NationalGeographic.com)

## HABITAT

Located:         North America, Asia, and Europe
Terrain:         Wooded, close to streams
Climate:         In the wintertime, temperatures stay below freezing. During the spring, it gets warmer. In the summer, highs are in the sixties and seventies.
Sleep:           Grizzly bears live in dens that are made in hollow trees, holes they dig, or caves so they can hibernate during the winter.
Other animals:   Moose, bison, pronghorn antelope, deer, coyotes, wolves, trumpeter swans, eagles, elk

## PREDATORS

Coyotes, wolves, and other bears are predators of the grizzly bear.

## DIET

Omnivore (eats both plants and animals)

Since grizzly bears are omnivores, their diet includes nuts, berries, fruit, leaves, and roots as well as other animals, such as rodents, moose, and salmon.

## BABIES

Mothers give birth during winter hibernation and usually have two cubs at a time. They are blind and hairless, weighing 8.5 to 11.5 ounces, about the size of a chipmunk. They will stay with their mother through the following winter season.

Grizzly mothers are very protective of their young and can become very dangerous to humans and any other animal that comes between them and their cubs.

## INTERESTING FACTS

- "The grizzly bear obtained its name because of the grayish/grizzled tips of its fur." (NationalGeographic.com)
- "Grizzly bears can run up to 30 mph." (NationalGeographic.com)
- Female grizzlies are call sows.

# GRIZZLY BEAR HUNT

This hunt is going to take place in Yellowstone National Park in Wyoming in the month of June. All information and statistics come, verbatim, from the World Factbook (Central Intelligence Agency) as well as the US Census Bureau in September 2010:

| | |
|---|---|
| Continent: | North America |
| Conventional long form: | United States of America |
| Conventional short form: | United States |
| State: | Wyoming |
| Capital city: | Cheyenne |
| Population: | 544,270 (2009 est.) |
| Languages: | English 82.1%, Spanish 10.7%, Indo-European 3.8%, Asian and Pacific Island 2.7%, other 0.7% (2000 census) |
| Currency: | US dollar |
| Geographic coordinates: | 38° 00' N, 97° 00' W |
| Location: | North America bordering both the North Atlantic Ocean and the North Pacific Ocean, between Canada and Mexico. In the United States of America, Wyoming is south of Montana, east of Idaho, northeast of Utah, north of Colorado, northeast of Nebraska, and southeast of South Dakota |

## Students close their eyes, and the teacher explains what Yellowstone National Park looks like.

Think about a place that has a lot of beautiful trees and mountains. You can see steam coming from geysers and hear the water bubbling. Listen carefully and you may be able to hear waterfalls and fast-moving water in streams. If you look hard enough, you can see moose, deer, bison, and perhaps a beautiful eagle flying above you.

## Students open their eyes and the hunt begins.

Well, here we are again, time to go on another hunt. This time we're hunting grizzly bears. And we're going to a very popular place called Yellowstone National Park in Wyoming, where animals can live in nature.

Are we ready? No, not yet? Oh yeah, we need to make sure we have everything we need.

Camera? Check.
Hat? Check.
Good hiking boots? Check.
Walking stick? Check.
Binoculars? Check.
Don't forget to kiss Mom! Check.

Do you know what? I think we should take the jeep, because we have to drive a little way. Are you ready? I'm ready. Let's go!

## RUN TO THE JEEP/HOP IN THE JEEP

**RUMMMBBLLLEEE STOP** Look over there by those trees. That animal looks a little familiar. It's not very big. It looks like a cat with tufts on its ears and a black-spotted tail with a white tip. Oh, I remember what it is. It's a bobcat! I think it's really cute. Want to take a picture? Okay, but I think we'd better take it from here and not get too close. Ready? **CLICK** Okay, I think we should continue looking for a grizzly bear.

**RUMMMBBLLLEEE STOP** Okay, I think it's time to get out and go for a hike. Ready?

**WALK STOP** Wow! I see a deer. Do you? Wait a minute. That's not a deer; it's an antelope! It has horns and a head like a deer, but it is shaped a little differently. It is wider than a deer. Well, let's get going so we can find a grizzly bear.

**WALK** Look up! Oh, what a beautiful bird. It has a white head, a large wingspan, and black feathers with white on its tail. Do you know what this bird is? It's an American bald eagle. Cool! I would like to take another picture. Are you ready? **CLICK** I think we'd better keep on walking. I haven't seen a grizzly bear yet.

**WALK STOP** Look over there! Let's get our binoculars. I think I see—yep, it's a grizzly bear! Let's get a closer. It's brown and furry with big claws. Oh, it must be a mama because there are two really cute cubs next to her. They look like they're boxing. I'm so happy we found them! Yeah! Woo-hoo! Oops, I think we woo-hooed too loudly and bothered the grizzly bear. How do I know? Because it's coming this way! Guess what time it is. It's running time! **RUN**

---

To end the hunt, lead the students in repeating the movements in reverse order without talking. This must be done quickly, as if they're afraid they will be caught.

Then, end safely back at the start and give Mom a big kiss.

# KOALA

## DESCRIPTION

| | |
|---|---|
| Type: | Mammal (marsupial, which means "pouched mammal") |
| Weight: | 10–30 lbs. |
| Height: | 2–3 feet |
| Color: | Light gray to brown with white on its neck, chest, and ears |
| Intelligence: | Not of high intelligence |
| Head: | Large head with small eyes and a big nose |
| Tail: | No tail |
| Claws: | Five fingers with claws (two opposable fingers) and five toes with claws (one opposable thumb that does not have a claw on it). |
| Texture: | Fur is woolly, soft, and dense |
| Movement: | Walks and runs on four legs |
| Smell: | Very good sense of smell |
| Hearing: | Keen sense of hearing |
| Sight: | Poor sense of sight |
| Life span: | 13–20 years in the wild |

Size relative to a six-foot man:
(NationalGeographic.com)

## HABITAT

| | |
|---|---|
| Terrain: | Eucalyptus forests |
| Climate: | Hot humid summers/dry mild winters |
| Sleep: | In trees—Females active at night, inactive during day; Males more active and feed during the day as well as at night |
| Other Animals: | Tasmanian devils, kangaroos, wallabies |

## PREDATORS

Several different animals prey on koalas, including goannas, dingoes, powerful owls, wedge-tailed eagles, and pythons.

## DIET

Herbivore (plant eater)

Koalas eat the leaves of eucalyptus trees. Of the more than six hundred kinds of eucalyptus, koalas eat forty to fifty different kinds. Of those, they really prefer about ten. They will also eat mistletoe and box leaves. Koalas can eat up to two and a half pounds of leaves each day.

Eucalyptus leaves are very poisonous, but due to the koalas' excellent sense of smell, they can determine which leaves are poisonous to their systems and which ones are not. Their digestive systems allow the breakdown of those that are not.

## BABIES

Baby koalas are called joeys. When they are first born, they do not have any hair or ears, are blind, and are about the size of a jellybean. Their development occurs while they are in their mothers' pouches for the first six months. Once developed, the joey will ride on its mother's back or cling to her belly. The joey stays with its mother wherever she goes for the first year of life.

## INTERESTING FACTS

- "The koala gets its name from an ancient Aboriginal word meaning "no drink" because it receives over 90% of its hydration from the Eucalyptus leaves (also known as gum leaves) it eats, and only drinks when ill or at times when there is not enough moisture in the leaves (i.e., during droughts, etc.)" (theKoala.com).
- 40% of its skull is fluid – known as one mammal whose brain does not fit their head.
- The "fur on the koala's bottom is densely packed to provide a 'cushion' for the hard branches it sits on, and has a 'speckled' appearance which makes koalas hard to spot from the ground." (theKoala.com)

# KOALA HUNT

This hunt is going to take place in Australia in the state and territory of Queensland, where the capital is Brisbane, in the month of September. All information and statistics come, verbatim, from the World Factbook (Central Intelligence Agency) website in September 2010:

Continent:                          Australia
Conventional long form:             Commonwealth of Australia
Conventional short form:            Australia
Population:                         21,262,641 (July 2010 est.)
Capital city:                       Canberra
Languages:                          English 78.5%, Chinese 2.5%, Italian 1.6%, Greek 1.3%, Arabic
                                    1.2%, Vietnamese 1%, other 8.2%, unspecified 5.7%
Currency:                           Australian dollar
Geographic coordinates:             27° 00' S, 133° 00' E
Location:                           Oceania, continent between the Indian Ocean and the South Pacific
                                    Ocean

## Students close their eyes, and the teacher explains what Brisbane looks like.
Think about a place that has a lot of beautiful, tall trees. It's very humid and hot. You can hear a lot of wild animals, like the Tasmanian devil's growl, or maybe you can hear a kangaroo jumping around you.

## Students open their eyes and the hunt begins.

Are you ready to find a cute little koala? I am! I think we're going to have a relaxing hunt this time. We are in Australia, so let's take some cool pictures. We have to wait until it gets a little darker because the koalas are more active during the night. Let's see if it's time to go. I'll look out my window.

**PULL BACK SHADE AND LOOK OUTSIDE** OK, I think it's time to go. Are you ready? We have to make sure we have everything we need.

Hat? Check.
Good hiking boots? Check.
Don't forget to kiss Mom! Check.

Do you know what I think we should do? Well, we're in Australia, so I think we should speak with an Australian accent. Can you say, "G'day, mate"? Oooh, very good. OK, let's get going.

**OPEN DOOR/SHUT DOOR**

**WALK STOP** Look at the big trees! Look at this branch. Oops, this branch is moving—plus it has a long tongue. Yikes! It's really a snake! I don't know about you, but I don't like snakes. Let's keep going.

**WALK STOP** Shine your flashlight over there. Huh? What do you mean we forgot our flashlight? Okay, let's go back. Just watch out for that snake!

**WALK OPEN DOOR** There's our flashlight. Oops, let's grab our camera too. We can't take pictures without a camera.

**SHUT THE DOOR WALK DUCK** That snake is getting lower. It gives me the shivers. **SHIVER**

**WALK STOP** What's that over there? It's hopping around like a jumping bean. Hey, that's not a jumping bean. It's a kangaroo! Cool! But there's something sticking out of its tummy. Oh, that's not just *anything*. That's a joey—a baby kanga. And that's not its stomach; it's a pouch! Picture opportunity! **CLICK** Okay, let's keep going. Got to find a koala.

**WALK STOP** Look up in that tree. Why, it's a koala! Yeah! We found one! Watch it eat. It's eating tree bark and eucalyptus leaves. How wonderful it is to watch them. Let's take some more pictures. **CLICK**

Do you know what I read? I read that there really is an animal called a Tasmanian devil. They are really cute. They look like little black bear cubs, but they are very dangerous. And guess where they live? Yep, right here in Australia. Well, I think it's time to go back. Ready? Let's go.

**WALK LISTEN** Did you hear that? It sounds like a snarling noise. *Snarling*? Wait a minute. Tasmanian devils snarl. No way. You don't think … It couldn't be … It's sounding a little closer. It's coming from over there.

**LOOK CLOSER** Oh, my! Not only is it snarling; it's showing its teeth. And they are big, sharp teeth! Yes! It *is* a Tasmanian devil. Yikes! Let's get out of here! **RUN**

---

To end the hunt, lead the students in repeating the movements in reverse order without talking. This must be done quickly, as if they're afraid they will be caught.

Then, end safely back at the start and give Mom a big kiss.

# POLAR BEAR

## DESCRIPTION

| | |
|---|---|
| Type: | Mammal |
| Weight: | 900 to 1,600 lbs. (females are smaller than males) |
| Height: | 8–11 feet tall |
| Color: | White |
| Intelligence: | They are very smart |
| Head: | Small |
| Tail: | Flat and small, about 3–5 inches long |
| Paws: | Wide and partly webbed toes (to help them swim); paws as big as twelve inches in diameter—front paws used for paddling; back paws used for steering |
| Texture: | Thick fur |
| Movement: | Walks, runs, and swims using two or four legs |
| Smell: | Very good sense of smell |
| Sight: | Very good, a lot like humans' |
| Hearing: | Very good, a lot like humans' |
| Taste: | Unclear if their sense of taste determines what foods they eat |
| Life span: | 25–30 years in the wild |

Size relative to a six-foot man:
(NationalGeographic.com)

## HABITAT

| | |
|---|---|
| Located: | Icy arctic areas of North America, Europe, and Russia |
| Terrain: | Snowy, glaciers |
| Climate: | Icy arctic areas |
| Sleep: | They sleep in dens and spend between seven and eight hours each night sleeping, as well as take naps during the day. |
| Other animals: | Moose, white-tailed deer, wolves, loons (bird) |

## PREDATORS

Polar bears don't really have any predators. Adult males may kill each other when competing for females, but not very often. During the first year of life, cubs are vulnerable and can be killed by wolves.

## DIET

Carnivores (meat eater)

Polar bears spend a lot of time in the water, which is also where they catch their prey. They like to eat seals, some walruses, fish, and carcasses of whales.

## BABIES

Mother polar bears build dens made out of snow. They will stay there during the winter. During this time, they will give birth to two cubs. The cubs will live with their mother for a little over two years, until they have learned survival skills.

## INTERESTING FACTS

- "Under the fur, polar bears have black skin, which helps hold in heat from the sun." (NationalGeographic.com)
- "The polar bear is the world's largest carnivore." (MontanaBears.com)
- They can smell prey twenty miles away.
- They do not drink water.
- Both the thick and woolly fur, as well as the guard fur, are clear. The core reflects light which make their fur look white.
- They have two different kinds of fur. One kind is thick, woolly and lies close to the skin, which helps keep them warm. The other type of fur are shaped like hollow straws (known as guard hairs) which acts as a protection so the bear's skin doesn't get wet.
- Front paws used for paddling; back paws used for steering

# POLAR BEAR HUNT

This hunt is going to take place in Manitoba, Canada, during the winter. All information and statistics come, verbatim, from the World Factbook (Central Intelligence Agency) website in September 2010:

| | |
|---|---|
| Continent: | North America |
| Conventional long form: | None |
| Conventional short form: | Canada |
| Population: | 487,208 (July 2010 est.) |
| Capital city: | Ottawa |
| Languages: | English (official) 58.8%, French (official) 21.6%, other 19.6% (2006 Census) |
| Currency: | Canadian dollar |
| Geographic coordinates: | 60° 00' S, 95° 00' E |
| Location: | Northern North America, bordering the North Atlantic Ocean on the east, North Pacific Ocean on the West and the Arctic Ocean on the north, north of the continental U.S. |

## Students close their eyes, and the teacher explains what Manitoba, Canada, looks like during the winter.

Think about a place that is rural and very cold with a lot of snow and ice. You might see wolves, moose, and even loons. Listen closely and you may hear a wolf growling or a loon singing.

## Students open their eyes and the hunt begins.

We're going on a hunt—a polar bear hunt. We're going to Canada, actually Manitoba, Canada, where the polar bears live. It's going to be cold, so we'd better get ready.

Camera? Check.
Winter coat? Check.
Warm boots? Check.
Snow shoes? Check.
Kiss my mom? Check.

**OPEN DOOR/SHUT DOOR**

**SWOOSH STOP** It's so cold that I can see my breath. Let's look.

**BREATHE** That's cool! It looks like steam is coming out of your mouth. Okay, let's go.

**SWOOSH** Look at all the beautiful snow. It looks like a winter wonderland..

**STOP** What's that? It looks like a dog. It's so beautiful. Let's get closer. Oops, maybe not. It has long, sharp teeth. I don't think it's a dog; it's a wolf! OK, let's quietly swoosh away.

**SWOOSH STOP** Wow! Did you hear that? Look up in the sky. I see a big bird. It's as big as a Canadian goose, but it's not that. It's black and white with red eyes. Wait a minute. Did you see it dive into the water? What did it come up with? Ooh, it got a fish to eat! This bird is called a loon. Do you know what I want to do? Yep, it's time to take a picture. Ready? **CLICK** You know what? I would like to keep going so that I can find a polar bear. Ready? Let's go.

**SWOOSH** Oops, we have a little hill to climb. Let's go. I know we can make it. (Keep swooshing and make grunting noises like it's difficult to climb.) Whew! We made it! Let's keep going.

**SWOOSH STOP** Look over there. I think my eyes are playing tricks on me! **RUB EYES** It looks so white out here that it looks like the snow is moving. Wait a minute. That moving snow has dark eyes, and it's standing up. It has a *big* mouth with ferocious teeth, has big claws, and is looking a little hungry. Uh, it's moving toward me. It's a polar bear! I think it's time to swoosh quickly! **RUN**

---

To end the hunt, lead the students in repeating the movements in reverse order without talking. This must be done quickly, as if they're afraid they will be caught.

Then, end safely back at the start and give Mom a big kiss.

# SIBERIAN TIGER

## DESCRIPTION

Type:           Mammal
Weight:         900–1025 lbs.
Height:         3.5 feet
Length:         5-13 feet
Color:          Thin black stripes, with orange on top that fades into white toward the bottom; lighter during the winter (helps blend in with the snow)
Intelligence:   Very intelligent
Head:           Not very big; two ears, two white patches over the eyes, and sensory whiskers
Tail:           Around three feet long
Claws:          Retractable
Texture:        Thick and coarse
Movement:       Walks and runs on four legs
Smell:          Very good sense of smell
Hearing:        Excellent
Sight:          Excellent
Life span:      Twenty-five years in the wild

Size relative to a six-foot man:
(NationalGeographic.com)

## HABITAT

Located:        Asia/Europe
Terrain:        Woodlands
Climate:        Winters = Black Sea coast is mild. It is colder in the northwest and inland areas. Siberia is freezing. Summers = West and central are balmy to warm. North and arctic coasts are cooler.
Sleep:          They can sleep anywhere from eighteen to twenty hours a day. They will sleep anywhere they want. They will sleep on rocks, in grass, or even next to their prey.
Other Animals:  Long-horned goats, ibex, musk deer, polar bears, seals, walrus, wolves, ermines, red-breasted geese, ducks, lemmings, several other burrowing animals, small lynx, and arctic foxes.

## PREDATORS

The Siberian tiger is at the top of the food chain and has no natural predators other than humans.

## DIET

Carnivore (meat eater)

These tigers can eat up to sixty pounds of food in one night. They will eat elk, deer, wild boar, and bear.

## BABIES

There are normally two to six cubs per litter, and they weigh about two pounds each. Cubs stay with their mother for approximately two to three years. At eight weeks old, they learn how to hunt from their mother, but do not hunt on their own until they are eighteen months old.

## INTERESTING FACTS

- "Siberian (or Amur) tigers are the world's largest cats." (NationalGeographic.com)
- Their eyes can reflect light, which gives them night vision that is six times better than that of humans.
- They have extra fur on their paws, during the winter, to help keep them warm. During the summer, their fur is much shorter.

# SIBERIAN TIGER HUNT

This hunt is going to take place in Siberia, Russia, in the month of July. All information and statistics come, verbatim, from the World Factbook (Central Intelligence Agency) website in September 2010:

| | |
|---|---|
| Continent: | Asia |
| Conventional long form: | Russian Federation |
| Conventional short form: | Russia |
| Population: | 140,041,247 (July 2010 est.) |
| Capital city: | Moscow |
| Languages: | Russian, many minority languages |
| Currency: | Russian ruble |
| Geographic coordinates: | 60° 00' S, 100° 00' E |
| Location: | Northern Asia (the area west of the Urals is considered part of Europe), bordering the Arctic Ocean, between Europe and the North Pacific Ocean. |

## Students close their eyes, and the teacher explains what Siberia looks like.

Think about a place that is beautiful. Look around, and you can see streams flowing next to the grasslands. All around you are beautiful hills and mountains. The temperature is perfect, about seventy degrees.

## Students open their eyes and the hunt begins.

We're going on a hunt, a Siberian tiger hunt. Do you know where? We're going to Russia, of course. To be more specific, Siberia, Russia. It is a very beautiful place, but it can get very cold—actually freezing—during the winter. But we're here in the summer, so we won't get cold. The weather is just right! Are you ready? Well, let's make sure we have everything we need.

Hiking boots? Check.
Water bottles? Check.
Backpacks? Check.
Hats? Check.
Camera? Check.
Kiss our moms? Check.

Ready? Let's go.

**OPEN DOOR/SHUT DOOR**

**WALK** Do you know what? I think I want to take our jeep.

**JUMP IN THE JEEP RUMMMBBLLLEEE STOP** Look all around. I wonder if we will see any wildlife.

**RUMMMBBLLLEEE STOP** I think that we'd better hike from here so we can get up close and personal with the animals. Well, maybe not *that* close, but close enough.

**WALK STOP** What is that? It looks like it has very long, skinny legs, a long beak, and some feathers. I've seen these before on a commercial at home—you know, those Vlasic pickle commercials? It's one of those birds that deliver babies on cartoons. Now what are they called? That's right—storks. Since this one is black, I bet it's called a black stork. Let's take a picture. **CLICK** Okay, let's keep looking for the Siberian tiger.

**WALK STOP** I hear something familiar. It sounds like something is quacking. What could that be? I'm thinking it's some kind of duck, but what kind? Let's go find out.

**WALK** Hey, it's sounds like it's getting closer. There's water over there. Let's go look. Wow! Look at that duck! Actually, it's a mandarin duck. I know that it's a male because it has very bright, beautiful colors. The female's colors are much softer, with little bits of gray, brown, and white. Do you know what I want to do? That's right—take a picture. **CLICK** Okay, let's keep going.

**WALK** Yikes! I hear a *big* snore. I wonder what that is. Wait! Look over by that tree. I see something black, big, and furry rubbing up and down on that tree. It must have an itch. It must have a big bear itch because it's an Asian bear. I think we should leave it alone to scratch its back. Let's tiptoe so we don't disturb it.

**TIPTOE STOP** I hear something cute. It's a tiny little growl. Should I get a little closer? Why not? It doesn't sound dangerous.

**TIPTOE** Look! It is too cute! It looks like a little baby tiger. I bet I can pet it like my cat TigerLilly. What do you think? Are you ready to get closer? No? Why are you saying no? *What?* You hear a bigger growl? Really? Let me check.

**TURN AROUND** Oh, my! I think you are absolutely correct, and I think it's time to run! **RUN**

---

To end the hunt, lead the students in repeating the movements in reverse order without talking. This must be done quickly, as if they're afraid they will be caught.

Then, end safely back at the start and give Mom a big kiss.

# TYRANNOSAURUS REX

## DESCRIPTION

Type:          Prehistoric
Weight:        5 to 7 tons
Height:         15 to 20 feet
Length:        40 feet
Color:          Unknown (not yet determined by scientists)
Intelligence:    Could process visual information
Head:           Had a massive head that was five feet long with a four-foot-long jaw; eye sockets four inches across (would have made the eyeballs approximately three inches in diameter)
Neck:           Short and muscular
Arms:          Small compared to the rest of the body, only three feet long
Tail:            Stiff and pointed; helped maintain balance
Feet:           About three feet long with three large toes and a dewclaw (a very tiny fourth toe) on each foot
Texture:       Rough, scaly skin that felt bumpy, like an alligator's skin, but has been described as "lightly pebbled skin"
Movement:    Walked and ran on two legs
Smell:         Was able to process odors
Sight:         Had the ability to perceive depth
Life span:     Best guess to date is approximately forty years

Size relative to a bus:
(NationalGeographic.com)

## HABITAT

Located:       North America and Asia
Terrain:       Open forests with nearby rivers and coastal forested swamps
Climate:      Humid, semitropical environment
Sleep:         Again, another best guess is that the T. rex probably slept like a horse, standing up. It had something called a "big pubic boot," which was a bone in its pelvis.
Other Animals: albertosaurus, anatosarus anectens (formerly called trachodon), triceratops, pterodactyl, kronosaurus (marine reptile), carnotaurus, brontosaurus

## PREDATORS

The only known natural rivals were other T-rexes.


## DIET

Carnivore (meat eater)

Their preys were mainly plant-eating dinosaurs, such as triceratops.


## BABIES

There's no real evidence that the T-rex, or other meat eaters, took care of their young. Some experts believe that perhaps they took care of the hatchlings for a small amount of time, just like most birds do.

No one knows what the T-rex's eggs looked like or how big they were, because no one has ever found one.


## INTERESTING FACTS

- "*Tyrannosaurus* means 'tyrant lizard.'" (NationalGeographic.com)
- They are believed to have run up to fifteen miles per hour and to make quick turns while running.
- Even though the T-rex's body was strong, its bones were hollow.

# TYRANNOSAURUS REX HUNT

This hunt is going to take place in a local museum.

## Students close their eyes, and the teacher explains what a museum looks like.
Think about a building that has a lot of wonderful things to see. Then think about what the room with prehistoric animals would be like. In your mind, look around at all the bones that make up these animals' skeletal systems.

## Students open their eyes and the hunt begins.

Okay, are you ready for another hunt? This one is going to be very exciting! Why? Because we get to go on a trip to the museum to see a Tyrannosaurus rex. Are you ready? Let's make sure we have everything we need.

Camera? Check.
Tickets? Check.
Good walking shoes? Check.
Kiss my mom? Gigantic T-rex check!

Let's get in the car.

**OPEN DOOR/SHUT DOOR**

**BROOOMMM STOP** Let's park over there.

**SCREECH OPEN DOOR/SHUT DOOR**

**WALK HAND TICKETS TO THE GUIDE** Okay, let's go to the dinosaur exhibit.

**WALK** There it is.

**WALK STOP** Wow! There are a lot of dinosaurs in here, but I want to see the mighty T-rex. Wait. Look over there in the middle of the room. Wow! It is really big!

I wonder what it was really like back sixty-five million years ago. I bet if we close our eyes, we can imagine what it was like.

**CLOSE YOUR EYES** Wait a minute. Did you hear that? I hear a lot of different noises—nothing like what I should be hearing in a museum. Huh, I hear screeching roars. Whoa! Did you feel that? It felt like the ground was moving. I think it's time to open our eyes.

**OPEN EYES** Oh, my word! I think we somehow went back in time. Look at all of the trees and forests. I hear water. Let's walk that way.

**WALK STOP** Look over there by that huge tree. I think it's a brontosaurus. Yep, it has a very long neck, and it's reaching up into the tree to eat some leaves. We don't have to worry about a brontosaurus. They're vegetarians and won't eat us. We just have to make sure we don't get in their way when they walk.

**SCREECH** Did you hear that? Look up. It looks like a huge flying bird. Uh, maybe a bat. It has a pointed head. Wait. I know that that is! It's a pterodactyl. I don't want to be way out here in the open. It may think we're tasty little morsels. Let's run toward a tree.

**RUN STOP** Wait a minute. Look over there in the forest. I think I see something moving. It has a huge head; sharp, pointed teeth; short arms; a long tail; birdlike feet; and quite an attitude. Do you know what? I think we found our T. rex! And I think it's time to go back home *now!* Quick! Close your eyes.

**CLOSE EYES** Say to yourself, "I want to be back in the museum." Oh no! I can feel the T-rex getting closer. Yikes! Wait. I don't hear the noises anymore. I hear people talking! Do you think we're back in the museum again? Should we open our eyes?

**OPEN EYES** Whew! We made it back. Oh, we must have been gone for a long time, because the museum is getting ready to close. Let's go home. I don't want my mom to get worried. Let's go!

---

To end the hunt, lead the students in repeating the movements in reverse order without talking. This must be done quickly, as if they're afraid they will be caught.

Then, end safely back at the start and give Mom a big kiss.

# VELOCIRAPTOR

## DESCRIPTION

Type:         Prehistoric
Weight:       75 pounds
Height:       1.6–3 feet
Length:       6–6.7 feet
Intelligence:  Considered an intelligent species due to its large brain (in proportion to its body)
Head:         About seven inches long
Neck:         S-shaped
Hands:       Three clawed fingers
Tail:           Long and stiff
Feet:          Four toes, the second toe being a retractable claw in the shape of a sickle that was at least three inches long
Texture:      feathed coat
Movement:   Stood upright; walked and ran on two legs
Life span:    Unknown

Size relative to a bus:
(NationalGeographic.com)

## HABITAT

Location:     North America and Asia
Terrain:      Streams, trees, and shrubs
Climate:     Desertlike environment
Other animals: Pinacosaurus, protoceratops

## PREDATORS

Apparently, animals only attacked the velociraptor when fighting to protect themselves. A famous fossil discovery was evidence of a fight between a velociraptor and a protoceratops. They were both killed at the same time—by a sandstorm, scientists think—and the fossils show the protoceratops holding onto the velociraptor's front foot while the velociraptor digs its sickle claw into the neck of the protoceratops.

## DIET

Carnivore (meat eaters)

Velociraptors would hunt in packs and form a triangle around their prey. They would eat anything they could take down, mainly herbivores.

## BABIES

The babies were hatched from eggs. Fossilized skulls indicate that young babies had proportionally shorter snouts and bigger eyes than the adults. It is thought that the young were taken care of by the adults for some time after hatching.

## INTERESTING FACTS

- "They may have been able to reach speeds of 24 miles an hour." (NationalGeographic. com)
- "Recent research suggests that *Velociraptor mongoliensis* was a feathered dinosaur. A forelimb fossil discovered in Mongolia showed quill knobs like those found in many modern birds. These telltale features are evidence of where ligaments attached flight feathers to bone and are considered proof that *Velociraptor* sported a fine feathery coat." (NationalGeographic. com)
- "They had hollow bones." (NationalGeographic.com)

# VELOCIRAPTOR HUNT

This hunt is going to take place in a child's backyard as the child plays with friends; the children will pretend they are in the prehistoric era.

## Students close their eyes, and the teacher explains what a backyard looks like.

Think about playing dinosaurs in your backyard. There is a lot of grass and a swing set over to the side. Look around at the other houses from your backyard. But all of a sudden, you don't hear the normal backyard noises anymore. You begin to hear strange noises. Those noises are growls from the Cretaceous Period. Look around. You don't see houses near your backyard anymore. What you see is a desertlike area with some streams.

## Students open their eyes and the hunt begins.

Are you ready? I said, are you ready? For what? Well, for a velociraptor hunt, of course!

We have to be very careful. There are some dangerous dinosaurs out there. Let's stay close together when we go. We have to check and make sure we have everything we need.

Camera? Check.
Hiking boots? Check.
Backpack? Check.
Most importantly, kiss my mom. Big check!

Okay, let's go.

**WALK STOP** Look over there. I think I see some bushes. Wow! Look behind that bush! That is a different-looking animal. It walks on four legs, and it looks like it has armor on its body. There is a club on its tail, and there are bony spikes along its back and tail. Wait a minute. I remember reading something on that. It is called a pinacosaurus. Can you say that three times fast? Pinacosaurus! Pinacosaurus! Pinacosaurus! That was hard. Anyway, we need to continue on. I really want to find a velociraptor.

**WALK STOP** Wait. I see something. It looks like—yes, it *looks* like a triceratops, but it's too small and doesn't have any horns. Let's get a closer look. Are you ready?

**WALK STOP** Okay, that's close enough. Look at it! It walks on four legs and has a body like a triceratops, but it's much smaller. It has a beak like a parrot's, and there is a bony frill on top of its head. Oh, yes, I know what that is. It's a protoceratops. I would like to get a picture. Are you ready?
**CLICK** Okay, I'm ready to find the velociraptor. Let's go.

**WALK** You know what? I'm getting the feeling that something is watching me. Are you getting the same feeling? You are!

**STOP** I hear a noise. It sounds like it's all around us. Oh, no. Do you know what? Velociraptors like to surround their prey. You don't think that … No, it couldn't be that. Perhaps they think that … *we're* the prey?

**BEND DOWN** I can feel them getting closer. The ground is shaking. Yikes! I feel … I feel … Wait! I feel a breeze, and I hear children playing. Are we back home? Should we open our eyes?

**OPEN EYES** Phew! We *are* back home. Let's get back into the house. Ready? **RUN**

---

To end the hunt, lead the students in repeating the movements in reverse order without talking. This must be done quickly, as if they're afraid they will be caught.

Then, end safely back at the start and give Mom a big kiss.

# KING COBRA

## DESCRIPTION

| | |
|---|---|
| Type: | Reptile |
| Group name: | Quiver |
| Weight: | Can weigh up to 20 pounds; a few up to 35 pounds |
| Length: | 12 to 18 feet long, with an average length of 13.4 feet |
| Color: | Adults: yellow, green, brown, or black with light yellow or a cream color on the throat area (color depends on the region they are from) |
| Juveniles: | black with yellow or white bars crossing their bodies |
| Intelligence: | High |
| Fangs: | Hollow and hold venom |
| Texture: | Scaly and looks wet but is actually dry to the touch |
| Movement: | Slithers |
| Smell: | Uses forked tongue |
| Sight: | Sighted; have good night vision |
| Hearing: | Can sense ground vibrations. |
| Taste: | With their forked tongue as well |
| Touch: | Feel through vibrations |
| Life span: | 20+ years in the wild. |

Size relative to a six-foot man
(NationalGeographic.com)

## HABITAT

| | |
|---|---|
| Located: | Southern Asia and Northern Africa |
| Terrain: | Dense jungle, cultivated fields, and forest areas where they can glide silently through undergrowth |
| Climate: | Rainy and humid with an average temperature of ninety-five degrees |
| Other animals: | Tigers, leopards, elephants, rhinoceros, wild buffalo, wild boar, deer, antelope, gibbons (small apes that live in trees), monkeys, flying foxes, wildcats, tapirs, crocodiles, pythons, geckos, turtles, exotic parrots, crows, pheasants, peafowl, paddybirds |

## PREDATORS

Natural predators of the king cobra include the mongoose, birds of prey, and man. King cobras are normally shy, but they will be aggressive when cornered and will stand their ground. The cobra will hiss at the intruder, raise its body up to about one third of its body length (around four to five feet in the air), spread its hood out, sway a little, and strike. They have also been known to spit venom in the eyes of their prey or intruder, which will sting and possibly kill them (if the venom gets into the bloodstream). On the cobra's hood, there are false eyespots that can make some predators afraid and cause them to stop their attack.

## DIET

Carnivore (meat eater)

They will eat other snakes (venomous and nonvenomous) as well as lizards, eggs, and small mammals, including rabbits, rats, and chicks. Since they are unable to chew, king cobras digest their prey with the strong acids in their stomachs.

## BABIES

King cobras are the only snakes that construct nests like birds. However, unlike birds, they build their nests on the ground for the only purpose of laying their eggs. They will lay twenty to forty eggs that will incubate for sixty-five to eighty days. When hatched, the hatchlings measure approximately eighteen inches in length and possess a bite that is deadly from day one.

The mother raises the young without any help from the father.

## SAFETY

If you do come across a king cobra, make sure that you do not corner it. Instead, give it space and back away from it slowly. Always make sure you learn about an area before exploring. It is also a good idea to have someone with you when you go exploring, especially someone who can serve as a guide.

## INTERESTING FACTS

- "Synthetic cobra venom is used in pain relievers and arthritis medication." (NationalGeographic.com)
- "They will also flare out their iconic hoods and emit a bone-chilling hiss that sounds almost like a growling dog." (NationalGeographic.com)
- "Although cobras can hear, they are actually deaf to ambient noises, sensing ground vibrations instead. The charmer's flute entices the cobra by its shape and movement, not by the music it emits." (NationalGeographic.com)
- King cobras are the longest of the venomous snakes.
- Cobras are the only snakes in the world that can spit their venom, and they are accurate up to a distance of about half their own length.

# KING COBRA HUNT

This hunt is going to take place in Burma, during its summertime. All information and statistics come, verbatim, from the World Factbook (Central Intelligence Agency) website in September 2010:

| | |
|---|---|
| Continent: | Asia |
| Conventional long form: | Union of Burma |
| Conventional short form: | Burma |
| Population: | 48,137,741 |
| Capital city: | Rangoon |
| Languages: | Burmese; minority ethnic groups have their own languages |
| Currency: | Australian dollar |
| Geographic coordinates: | 22° 00' S, 98° 00' E |
| Location: | Southeastern Asia, bordering the Andaman Sea and the Bay of Bengal, between Bangladesh and Thailand |

## Students close their eyes, and the teacher explains what Burma looks like.

Think about what Burma looks and feels like. It is a very hot and humid (sticky) place. It has steep hills, trees, and rivers and is very green. Listen to the different birds and roars of other animals, including tigers and elephants.

## Students open their eyes and the hunt begins.

Are you ready for a great hunt? You are? Well, let's get started. This time, we're going to hunt a cobra, but not just *any* cobra. We're hunting a king cobra. Yeah! Where, you ask? Why, we're going to Burma. It's located on the continent of Asia.

Well, let's get ready. Do I have my
Hat? Check.
Backpack? Check.
Camera? Check.
Water? Check.
Walking stick? Check.
Sunglasses? Check.
Hiking boots? Check.
Kiss my mom? Big, humongous check.

Okay, let's go!

**OPEN DOOR/SHUT DOOR** Instead of walking, let's take our jeep.

**JUMP IN THE JEEP**

**RUMMMBBLLLEEE STOP** What is that over there? Let's get out for a minute to get a closer look.

**JUMP OUT OF JEEP WALK STOP** Wow! Look at that! It has a black, furry body with a white, furry face and hands. It's really cute and reminds me of a cuddly monkey. Hey, do you know what? This is a gibbon, and they aren't monkeys. They're really small apes, but not like gorillas or anything like that. Whoa! Did you see that gibbon swing from tree to tree? It must have been going pretty quickly. Let's see if we can get a picture of it in midflight. There it goes! **CLICK** That was pretty cool, but we still need to find our king cobra. Ready? Let's go.

**WALK JUMP IN THE JEEP RUMMMBBLLLEEE STOP** Look at that huge animal with big floppy ears! I cannot remember the name. It's on the tip of my tongue. Wait. It has a very long trunk, and it's moving a tree. It has a pretty strong nose (ha, ha). I remember now—it's an elephant! Should we take a picture? Sure. Why not? **CLICK** You know what? I still want to find a king cobra. Let's keep going.

**RUMMMBBLLLEEE** Isn't this a beautiful place? Lots of trees and water. Wait!

**STOP** I see something in the water. It has a black beak and feathers. Its legs are kind of long, and it has a few stripes from its head to its tummy. Do you know what this is? It's an Indian pond heron. I like this bird, but I really want to find the king cobra. Let's keep searching.

**RUMMMBBLLLEEE STOP** I think we will need to walk from here, but be careful. King cobras like to hide under brush and spring up at you.

**TIPTOE SWISH** Hey, what was that noise? It was very quiet, but I'm beginning to get the heebie jeebies. **SHAKE** I wonder if we should start walking back to the jeep. I'm not sure that I want to find a king cobra anymore. Oops! I think it heard us because it's right behind us, and it's "hooded out," which means it's not happy with us. Let's move very slowly away from it and not spook it anymore. Maybe we can get away safely.

**TIPTOE** OK, I think we might be able to run! **RUN**

---

To end the hunt, lead the students in repeating the movements in reverse order without talking. This must be done quickly, as if they're afraid they will be caught.

Then, end safely back at the start and give Mom a big kiss.

# KOMODO DRAGON

## DESCRIPTION

| | |
|---|---|
| Type: | Reptile |
| Weight: | 330 lbs. |
| Length: | 10 feet |
| Color: | Varies; can camouflage themselves within their environment |
| Intelligence: | Very intelligent |
| Head: | Long and flat with a rounded snout |
| Tail: | Huge, muscular, and longer than the body |
| Feet: | Sharp claws on toes |
| Legs: | Bowed and short |
| Texture: | Scaly skin |
| Movement: | Walks and runs on four legs |
| Sight: | Very good; can see up to 980 feet away |
| Smell: | Excellent |
| Taste: | Uses its long, yellow, forked tongue |
| Hearing: | Not very good |
| Life span: | Thirty or more years in the wild |

Size relative to a six-foot man:
(NationalGeographic.com)

## HABITAT

| | |
|---|---|
| Terrain: | Hilly areas, rain forests, and grassy lowlands |
| Climate: | Hot and humid |
| Sleep: | During the night |
| Other animals: | Goats, deer, wild boars, monkeys |

## PREDATORS

Humans and other Komodo dragons are the dragon's only real predators.

## DIET

Carnivore (meat eater)

They will eat just about anything, including carrion (dead meat), deer, water buffalo, monkeys, as well as humans. Komodo dragons are very patient and will lie still, waiting for any prey to pass by, including other Komodo dragons. When the prey comes close, the dragon will spring and attack it. Once it bites, the bacteria from the dragon's mouth will kill the prey within twenty-four hours. The Komodo bite is so deadly because there are more than fifty strains of bacteria found in its saliva.

## BABIES

After digging a hole, the mother will lay twenty to forty eggs and then cover them with dirt. The hatchlings are sixteen inches long at birth, and they eat insects and live in the trees.

## INTERESTING FACTS

- "The dragons can run up to 11 miles an hour in short bursts." (NationalGeographic.com)
- "Komodo dragons are the heaviest lizards on Earth." (NationalGeographic.com)
- "A dragon can eat a whopping 80 percent of its body weight in a single feeding." (NationalGeographic.com)

# KOMODO DRAGON HUNT

This hunt is going to take place on Komodo Island, one of the Indonesian islands, during the month of October. All information and statistics come, verbatim, from the World Factbook (Central Intelligence Agency) website in September 2010:

| | |
|---|---|
| Continent: | Asia |
| Conventional long form: | Republic of Indonesia |
| Conventional short form: | Indonesia |
| Population: | 240,271,522 (July 2010 est.) |
| Capital city: | Jakarta |
| Languages: | Bahasa Indonesia (official, modified form of Malay), English, Dutch, and local dialects (the most widely spoken of which is Javanese) |
| Currency: | Indonesian rupiah |
| Geographic coordinates: | 5° 00' S, 120° 00' E |
| Location: | Southeastern Asia, archipelago between the Indian Ocean and the Pacific Ocean |

## Students close their eyes, and the teacher explains what Komodo Island looks like.

Think about a place that is hot and humid. It has a lot of greenery—tall, green grass and palm trees. Feel the warm breeze across your face. Listen and you can hear cows, wild boars (pigs), and birds.

## Students open their eyes and the hunt begins.

Guess what we're going to do? That's right. We're going on a great hunt. Do you know what we're hunting? We're hunting one of the most dangerous and largest lizards in the world. It's called a Komodo dragon, and it lives on the island of Komodo. It's exciting, but we have to make sure we have everything we need.

Camera? Check.
Hat? Check.
Good hiking boots? Check.
Walking stick? Check.
Don't forget to Kiss my Mom Check

Okay, let's go.

**OPEN DOOR/CLOSE DOOR**

**WALK STOP** Look over there in the water. I can see a head with horns in the shape of a crescent moon. Ooh, did you see it come out of the water? It has four long legs and a long tail, and it's gray and black. Ooh, I know what it is! It's a water buffalo! How cool. Guess what I want to do. That's right. I want to take a picture. **CLICK** Okay, let's keep going

**WALK STOP** I wonder if I can get a better look up in that tree over there. What do you think? Yes? OK, let's walk over to that tree.

**WALK WAIT** Do you hear that? It's a beautiful chirping sound. It sounds like it's coming from this lontar palm tree. This tree has round fruit on it that looks like grapes. It's a pretty tree. Look deeper. I can see a bird that looks a little like a dove with wings that are blue, green, purple, and very iridescent. How beautiful! It's called a Komodo Island bird. Yes, I know. It's time to take a picture. **CLICK** Let's find another tree; I really want to get a look from up above the ground. There's one over there. Let's go.

**WALK STOP** Let's climb.

**CLIMB UP LEAN OUT** I think I see something crawling on the other side of that bridge. Let's get a closer look.

**CLIMB DOWN WALK BRIDGE WALK STOP** There it is! That is one huge lizard! Should we get just a little closer? Okay, just a little closer, but be very careful.

**WALK STOP** I think we're close enough. Look at its big eyes. And talk about big—did you see it yawn? Did you see those teeth? It's looking a little hungry, and … uh, er, those big eyes are looking at me. I think we'd better run! **RUN**

---

To end the hunt, lead the students in repeating the movements in reverse order without talking. This must be done quickly, as if they're afraid they will be caught.

Then, end safely back at the start and give Mom a big kiss.

# APPENDIX – RELATED STATE TESTING MODULES (TEKS CHECKLIST)

## 2010–2011 TEXAS ESSENTIAL KNOWLEDGE AND SKILLS
## KINDERGARTEN

| Subject | Obj. | Description |
|---------|------|-------------|
| Science | K9.A | Differentiate between living and nonliving things based upon whether they have basic needs and produce offspring. |
| | K9.B | Examine evidence that living organisms have basic needs such as food, water, and shelter for animals. |
| Language Arts | K16.A | Understand and use the following parts of speech in the context of reading, writing and speaking (with adult assistance): (ii) nouns (singular/plural) and (iii) descriptive words. |
| | K16.B | Speak in complete sentences to communicate. |
| | K16.C | Use complete simple sentences. |
| | K21.A | Listen attentively by facing speakers and asking questions to clarify information. |
| | K21.B | Follow oral directions that involve a short related sequence of actions. |
| | K22 | Listening and Speaking/Speaking: Students speak clearly and to the point, using conventions of language. Students continue to apply earlier standards with greater complexity. Students are expected to share information and ideas by speaking audibly and clearly using the conventions of language. |
| Math | K10.A | Compare and order two or three concrete objects according to length (longer/shorter than, or the same). |
| | K10.D | Compare two objects according to weight/mass (heavier than, lighter than, equal to). |
| | K10.E | Compare situations or objects according to relative temperature (hotter/colder than, or the same as). |
| | K13.A | Identify mathematics in everyday situations. |
| | K13.D | Use tools such as real objects, manipulatives, and technology to solve problems. |
| Social Studies Skills | K4.A | Locate places using the four cardinal directions. |
| | K15.A | Obtain information about a topic using a variety of oral sources such as conversations, interviews, and music. |
| | K15.B | Obtain information about a topic using a variety of valid visual sources such as pictures, symbols, electronic media, printed material and artifacts. |
| | K15.C | Sequence and categorize information. |
| | K15.D | Identify main ideas from oral, visual and print sources. |
| | K16.A | Express ideas orally based on knowledge and experiences. |
| | K16.B | Create and interpret visuals including pictures and maps. |

# 2010–2011 TEXAS ESSENTIAL KNOWLEDGE AND SKILLS
## FIRST GRADE

| Subject | Obj. | Description |
|---|---|---|
| Science | 1.9A | Sort and classify living and nonliving things based upon whether or not they have basic needs and produce offspring. |
| | 1.9C | Gather evidence of interdependence among living organisms and animals using plants for shelter. |
| | 1.10A | Investigate how the external characteristics of an animal are related to where it lives, how it moves, and what it eats. |
| | 1.10C | Compare ways that young animals resemble their parents. |
| | 1.10D | Observe and record life cycles of animals. |
| Language Arts | 1.20A | Understand and use the following parts of speech in the context of reading, writing and speaking: (i) verbs (past, present, future); (ii) nouns (singular/plural, common/proper); (iii) adjectives (e.g., descriptive: green, tall); (iv) adverbs (e.g., time: before, next). |
| | 1.20B | Speak in complete sentences with correct subject-verb agreement. |
| | 1.20C | Ask questions with appropriate subject-verb inversion. |
| | 1.27A | Listen attentively to speakers and ask relevant questions to clarify information. |
| | 1.27B | Follow, restate and give oral instructions that involve a short related sequence of actions. |
| | 1.28 | Listening and Speaking/Speaking. Students speak clearly and to the point, using the conventions of language. Students continue to apply earlier standards with greater complexity. Students are expected to share information and ideas about the topic under discussion, speaking clearly at an appropriate pace, using the conventions of language. |
| | 1.3C | Ask and answer relevant questions and make contributions in small or large group discussions. |
| Math | 1.7B | Compare and order two or more concrete objects according to length (from longest to shortest). |
| | 1.7F | Compare and order two or more objects according to weight/mass (from heaviest to lightest). |
| | 1.7G | Compare and order two or more objects according to relative temperature (from hottest to coldest). |
| | 1.11A | Identify mathematics in everyday situations. |
| | 1.11D | Use tools such as real objects, manipulatives, and technology to solve problems. |
| Social | 1.4A | Locate places using the four cardinal directions. |
| Studies Skills | 1.5B | Locate places of significance on maps and globes such as the local community, Texas, and the United States. |
| | 1.17A | Obtain information about a topic using a variety of oral sources such as conversations, interviews, and music. |
| | 1.17B | Obtain information about a topic using a variety of visual sources such as pictures, graphics, television maps, computer images, literature and artifacts. |
| | 1.17C | Sequence and categorize information. |
| | 1.17D | Identify main ideas from oral, visual, and print sources. |
| | 1.18A | Express ideas orally based on knowledge and experiences. |

# 2010–2011 TEXAS ESSENTIAL KNOWLEDGE AND SKILLS
## SECOND GRADE

| Subject | Obj. | Description |
|---|---|---|
| Science | 2.9A | Identify the basic needs of animals. |
| | 2.9C | Compare and give examples of the ways living organisms depend on each other and on their environments. |
| | 2.10A | Observe, record and compare how the physical characteristics and behaviors of animals help them meet their basic needs. |
| | 2.10C | Investigate and record life cycle stages of animals. |
| Language Arts | 2.21A | Understand and use the following parts of speech in the context of reading, writing and speaking: (i) verbs (past, present, future); (ii) nouns (singular/plural, common/proper); (iii) adjectives (e.g., descriptive: old, wonderful; articles: a, an, the); (iv) adverbs (e.g., time: before, next; manner, carefully, beautifully). |
| | 2.21B | Use complete sentences with correct subject-verb agreement. |
| | 2.28A | Listen attentively to speakers and ask relevant questions to clarify information. |
| | 2.28B | Follow, restate and give oral instructions that involve a short related sequence of actions. |
| | 2.29 | Listening and Speaking/Speaking: Students speak clearly and to the point, using the conventions of language. Students continue to apply earlier standards with greater complexity. Students are expected to share information and ideas that focus on the topic under discussion, speaking clearly at an appropriate pace, using the conventions of language. |
| Math | 2.9A | Identify concrete models that approximate standard units of length and use them to measure length. |
| | 2.12A | Identify mathematics in everyday situations. |
| Social Studies Skills | 2.3A | Name several sources of information about a given period or event. |
| | 2.5A | Use symbols, find locations, and determine directions on maps and globes. |
| | 2.6A | Identify major landforms and bodies of water, including continents and oceans on maps and globes. |
| | 2.6B | Locate the community, Texas, the United States and selected countries on maps and globes. |
| | 2.6C | Compare information from different sources about places and regions. |
| | 2.17A | Obtain information about a topic using a variety of valid oral sources such as conversations, interviews and music. |
| | 2.17B | Obtain information about a topic using a variety of valid sources such as pictures, graphics, television maps, computer software, literature, reference sources and artifacts. |
| | 2.17D | Sequence and categorize information. |
| | 2.17E | Interpret oral, visual and print material by identifying the main idea, predicting and comparing and contrasting. |

# 2010–2011 TEXAS ESSENTIAL KNOWLEDGE AND SKILLS
## THIRD GRADE

| Subject | Obj | Description |
|---|---|---|
| Science | 3.9A | Observe and describe the physical characteristics of environments and how they support populations and communities within an ecosystem. |
| | 3.9C | Describe environmental changes where some organisms thrive and others perish or move to new locations. |
| | 3.10A | Explore how structures and functions of animals allow them to survive in a particular environment. |
| | 3.10B | Explore that some characteristics of organisms are inherited and recognize that some behaviors are learned in response to living in a certain environment. |
| | 3.10C | Investigate and compare how animals undergo a series of orderly changes in their diverse life cycles. |
| Language Arts | 3.22A | Use and understand the function of the following parts of speech in the context of reading, writing and speaking: (i) verbs (past, present, future); (ii) nouns (singular/plural, common/proper); (iii) adjectives (e.g., descriptive: wooden, rectangular; limiting: this, that; articles: a, an, the); (iv) adverbs (e.g., time: before, next; manner: carefully, beautifully); (vii) coordinating conjunctions (e.g., and, or , but). |
| | 3.22B | Use the complete subject and the complete predicate in a sentence. |
| | 3.22C | Use complete simple and compound sentences with correct subject-verb agreement. |
| | 3.29A | Listen attentively to speakers, ask relevant questions, and make pertinent comments. |
| | 3.29B | Follow, restate and give oral instructions that involve a series of related sequences of action. |
| | 3.30 | Listening and Speaking/Speaking. Students speak clearly and to the point, using the conventions of language. Students continue to apply earlier standards with greater complexity. Students are expected to speak coherently about the topic under discussion, employing eye contact, speaking rate, volume, enunciation and the conventions of language to communicate ideas effectively. |
| Math | 3.11A | Use linear measurement tools to estimate and measure lengths using standard units. |
| | 3.11D | Identify concrete models that approximate standard units/mass and use them to measure weight/mass. |
| | 3.14A | Identify the mathematics in everyday situations. |
| Social Studies Skills | 3.5A | Use cardinal and intermediate directions to locate places on maps and globes such as the Amazon River, Himalayan Mountains, and Washington, D.C. on maps and globes. |
| | 3.5B | Use a scale to determine the distance between places on maps and globes. |
| | 3.5C | Identify and use the compass rose, grid, and symbols to locate places on maps and globes. |
| | 3.17A | Express ideas orally based on knowledge and experiences. |
| | 3.17C | Use standard grammar, spelling, sentence structure, and punctuation. |

| Subject | Obj | Description |
|---|---|---|
| Science | 4.10A | Explore how adaptations enable organisms to survive in their environment. |
| | 4.10B | Demonstrate that some likenesses between parents and offspring are inherited, passed from generation to generation. |
| | 4.10C | Explore, illustrate, and compare life cycles in living organisms. |
| Language Arts | 4.20A | Use and understand the function of the following parts of speech in the context of reading, writing and speaking: (i) verbs (irregular verbs); (ii) nouns (singular/plural, common/proper); (iii) adjectives (e.g., descriptive, including purpose: sleeping bag, frying pan) and the comparative and superlative forms (e.g., fast, faster, fastest); (iv) adverbs (e.g., frequently: usually, sometimes, intensity: almost, a lot). |
| | 4.20B | Use the complete subject and the complete predicate in a sentence. |
| | 4.20C | Use complete simple and compound sentences with correct subject-verb agreement. |
| | 4.27A | Listen attentively to speakers, ask relevant questions, and make pertinent comments. |
| | 4.27B | Follow, restate and give oral instructions that involve a series of related sequences of actions. |
| | 4.28 | Listening and Speaking/Speaking. Students speak clearly and to the point, using the conventions of language. Students are expected to express an opinion supported by accurate information, employing eye contact, speaking rate, volume and enunciation, and the conventions of language to communicate ideas effectively. |
| Math | 4.14A | Identify the mathematics in everyday situations. |
| Social Studies Skills | 4.6A | Apply geographic tools, including grid systems, legends, symbols, scales and compass roses to construct and interpret maps. |
| | 4.7A | Describe a variety of regions in Texas and the Western Hemisphere such as political, population, and economic regions that result from patterns of human activity. |
| | 4.7B | Describe a variety of regions in Texas and the Western Hemisphere such as landform, climate, and vegetation regions that result from physical characteristics. |
| | 4.7C | Compare the regions of Texas with regions of the United States and other parts of the world. |
| | 4.22C | Organize and interpret information in outlines, reports, databases, and visuals including graphs, charts, timelines, and maps. |
| | 4.22F | Use appropriate mathematical skills to interpret social studies information such as maps and graphs. |
| | 4.23A | Use social studies terminology correctly. |
| | 4.23B | Incorporate main and supporting ideas in verbal and written communication. |
| | 4.23C | Express ideas orally based on research and experiences. |
| | 4.23E | Use standard grammar, spelling, sentence structure, and punctuation. |

# 2010–2011 TEXAS ESSENTIAL KNOWLEDGE AND SKILLS
## FIFTH GRADE

| Subject | Obj | Description |
|---|---|---|
| Science | 5.9A | Observe the way organisms live and survive in their ecosystem by interacting with the living and non-living elements. |
| | 5.9C | Predict the effects of changes in ecosystems caused by living organisms. |
| | 5.9D | Identify the significance of the carbon dioxide-oxygen cycle to the survival of animals. |
| | 5.10A | Compare the structures and functions of different species that help them live. |
| | 5.10B | Differentiate between inherited traits of animals. |
| | 5.10C | Describe the differences between complete and incomplete metamorphosis. |
| Language Arts | 5.20A | Use and understand the function of the following parts of speech in the context of reading, writing and speaking. (i) verbs (irregular verbs and active voice); (ii) collective nouns (e.g., class, public); (iii) adjectives (e.g., descriptive, including origins: French windows, American cars and their comparative and superlative forms [e.g., good, better, best]); (iv) adverbs (e.g., frequency: usually, sometimes; intensity: almost, a lot). |
| | 5.20B | Use the complete subject and the complete predicate in a sentence. |
| | 5.20C | Use complete and compound sentences with correct subject-verb agreement. |
| | 5.27A | Listen to and interpret a speaker's message (both verbal and nonverbal) and ask questions to clarify the speaker's purpose or perspective. |
| | 5.27B | Follow, restate and give oral instructions that include multiple action steps. |
| Math | 5.14A | Identify the mathematics in everyday situations. |
| Social Studies Skills | 5.6A | Apply geographic tools, including grid systems, legends, symbols, scales, compass roses, to construct and interpret maps. |
| | 5.6B | Translate geographic data into a variety of formats such as raw data to graphs and maps. |
| | 5.7B | Describe a variety of regions in the United States, such as landforms, climate, and vegetation regions, that result from physical characteristics. |
| | 5.7C | Locate the fifty states on a map and identify regions such as New England and the Great Plains made up of various groups of states. |
| | 5.25C | Organize and interpret information in outlines, reports, databases and visuals including graphs, charts, timelines and maps. |
| | 5.26A | Use social studies terminology correctly. |
| | 5.26B | Incorporate main and supporting ideas in verbal and written communication. |
| | 5.26C | Express ideas orally based on research and experiences. |
| | 5.26E | Use standard grammar, spelling, sentences structure, and punctuation. |

# RESOURCES

## African Elephant
nationalgeographic.com (pulled data on 1/17/10)
wikipedia.org (pulled data on 1/17/10)
elephant.elehost.com (pulled data on 1/17/10)
cia.gov (pulled data on 9/12/10)
defenders.org (pulled data on 1/23/11)

## American Bison
nationalgeographic.com (pulled data on 12/15/09)
defenders.org (pulled data on 12/15/09)
cia.gov (pulled data on 9/12/10)
factfinder2.census.gov (pulled data on 9/12/10)

## Blue Mountain (Rainbow) Lorikeets
avianweb.com (pulled data on 12/15/09)
cia.gov (pulled data on 9/12/10)

## Cheetah
wikipedia.org (pulled data on 12/01/09)
nationalgeographic.com (pulled data on 12/01/09)
exzooberance.com (pulled data on 12/01/09)
cia.gov (pulled data on 9/12/10)

## Emperor Penguin
nationalgeographic.com (pulled data on 1/17/10)
antarcticconnection.com (pulled data on 1/17/10)
cia.gov (pulled data on 9/12/10)

## Great White Shark
nationalgeographic.com (pulled data on 1/17/10)
wikipedia.org (pulled data on 1/17/10)
cia.gov (pulled data on 9/12/10)

## Grizzly Bear
nationalgeographic.com (pulled data on 12/07/09)
wikipedia.org (pulled data on 12/07/09)
gov.bc.ca (pulled data on 12/07/09)
americansouthwest.net (pulled data on 12/07/09)
cia.gov (pulled data on 9/12/10)
factfinder2.census.gov (pulled data on 9/12/10)
montanabears.com (pulled data on 1/23/11)

## Hammerhead Shark
nationalgeographic.com (pulled data on 12/08/09)
wikipedia.org (pulled data on 12/08/09)
divingwithsharks.com (pulled data on 12/08/09)

cia.gov (pulled data on 9/12/10)
factfinder2.census.gov (pulled data on 9/12/10)

## King Cobra

nationalgeographic.com (pulled data on 11/21/09)
blueplanetbiomes.org (pulled data on 11/21/09)
cia.gov (pulled data on 9/12/10)

## Koala

nationalgeographic.com (pulled data on1/09/10)
wikipedia.org (pulled data on1/09/10)
exzooberance.com (pulled data on1/09/10)
cia.gov (pulled data on 9/12/10)

## Komodo Dragon

nationalgeographic.com (pulled data on 12/07/09)
wonderclub.com (pulled data on 12/07/09)
wikipedia.org (pulled data on 12/07/10)
cia.gov (pulled data on 9/12/10)

## Octopus

nationalgeographic.com (pulled data on 1/17/10)
wikipedia.org (pulled data on 1/17/10)
exzooberance.com (pulled data on 1/17/10)
cia.gov (pulled data on 9/12/10)
factfinder2.census.gov (pulled data on 9/12/10)

## Polar Bear

blueplanetbiomes.org (pulled data on 12/31/09)
montanabears.com (pulled data on 12/31/09)
nationalgeographic.com (pulled data on 12/31/09)
polarbearsinternational.org (pulled data on 12/31/09)
cia.gov (pulled data on 9/12/10)

## Siberian Tiger

nationalgeographic.com (pulled data 1/13/10)
wikipedia.org (pulled data on 1/13/10)
koreanhistoryproject.org (pulled data on 1/13/10)
avianweb.com (pulled data on 1/13/10)
cia.gov (pulled data on 9/12/10)

## Tyrannosaurus Rex

nationalgeographic.com (pulled data on 12/12/09)
wikipedia.org (pulled data on12/12/09)

## Velociraptor

nationalgeographic.com (pulled data on 12/12/09)
wikipedia.org (pulled data on12/12/09)

# ABOUT THE AUTHOR

Deborah A. Johnston has served in the education system for over eight years. Her passion is working in the special education department with elementary students. She enjoys looking for unique ways to teach children the skills they need, which led her to creating the *Hunting Trips in the Classroom* teacher's manual.